Around
the next
Corner

Around
the next
Corner

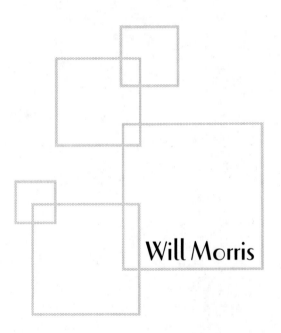

Will Morris

Printed in the United States of America.

ISBN 10: 1-59571-145-7
ISBN 13: 978-1-59571-145-8
Library of Congress Control Number: 2006929359

Word Association Publishers
205 5th Avenue
Tarentum, PA 15084
www.wordassociation.com

These recorded thoughts are dedicated to a very special lady, who has given more joy to my life than I have ever deserved.

Acknowledgments

Pages do not provide the space necessary to acknowledge the multitude of persons that have made these stories possible and my life so fruitful. I can only acknowledge my gratitude to God, who knows each of them.

January 13, 2008

Phil,

Thanks for our phone visit.
May your travel around the
next corner always be pleasant!

Wil

Table of Contents

Preface: Thoughts of a Traveler   11
1. Accidental and Unexpected   15
2. The Birth of a Merchant   19
3. Hasan Davis   24
4. The Accident of Birth   30
5. Dr. Dave   38
6. Tourist or Traveler   47
7. Flight Training   56
8. Smooth Gin Martini   64
9. Just Plain Dad   70
10. Lost Power   75
11. People Don't Smile   79
12. Wanda   85
13. Tenth Birthday Party   94
14. Hateful Defiance   102
15. Return to Helmstedt   107
16. Alice   115
17. Ronald Kidd   124
18. Rho Wang   130
19. Pharmacist   136
20. Sight   142
21. God's Language Barrier   146
22. Another Audience   150
23. The Sign by the Road   157
24. Visa Debit Card   161
25. The Party   169
26. George   175
27. Ephesus   181
28. Stanford Lee   185
29. Rae Elizabeth Pugh   194
30. Parker   199

Preface

Thoughts of a Traveler

My life has spanned more than three quarters of a century and has been, for me, an interesting journey, including my youth, school, military service, college, marriage, rearing a family, a career in retail, and now retirement. Each segment of the journey, except marriage, had an ending with its share of memories, but the next period always brought new and even more exciting experiences. Retirement, for me, has not been the beginning of the end of my life, but the beginning of a new life. Mortgages have been paid; children are through college and married; the morning alarm no longer signals it's time to go to the office. Retirement has been a time to reflect and remember yesterday, but more importantly, to look forward to and experience tomorrow.

I can best describe it as just going "around the next corner." Many unique people, places and circumstances have been part of this time of my life. I have piloted and jumped out of planes, hiked the C&O Canal, and traveled to more than fifty countries—meeting new and interesting friends on every step of the journey.

My wife's passion to add a college degree to her credentials as a registered nurse continued after our retirement and took us both around another corner. During our marriage and relocations around the country she had attended four different colleges. Career transfers, having children and just the business of life had prevented her from finishing. Our retirement provided her the opportunity to enroll at Chatham College in Pittsburgh for a very intensified eighteen months of study. Returning to the academic world at the age of sixty-two required hours and hours of concentration and study. There was little that I could do to help and I'm not sure that I didn't get in the way. The "corner" was an article in the *New York Times* about going around the world. My childhood fascination with the story of Magellan traveling around the world resurfaced, and I found myself with a camp stove, a tent, and a backpack, and fifty-two weeks traveling to fifty countries around this great planet we call earth. I returned the week she graduated.

I often find myself, "sitting on a rock," talking to people about their lives and circumstances. Most of these people feel totally unimportant in their world, and it has been my good fortune that they accept me as just another unimportant person and freely tell me their stories. As I listen to who they are, where they are and their own personal stories, I often allow my imagination to question what circumstances brought them to this place in their lives.

Life—anyone's life—can be compared to a motion picture: a long film made up of many frames. My contact with the people and their stories I share took place within one of the small frames of their lives. The story within that frame is a story within itself. As I journeyed through my own life, circumstances placed me at given points at given times. These experiences just happened. They were not planned. They might even be considered accidents.

A friend once referred to me as unique. Many of my experiences have been unusual, and they have been shared with a wide spectrum of personalities. But then, every person I've ever met is unique. There are no ordinary people in our world. You, as the reader, are unique and you will read these stories about unique people and my short encounters with them. I hope that you will find these stories enjoyable, or even fascinating. Perhaps they will allow you to engage the mind and circumstances of these people that you have not known. If they give you a broader view of our world, these stories will benefit both you and me.

Accidental and Unexpected

June 1943

1

In the rural farmland of Ohio, the nine miles to the county seat and three miles to the small village where I went to school measured the parameters of my world. Scholastically, I was in the lowest quarter of my eighteen-member class—except in math. In sports I never earned the right to wear a uniform. My vision for life was to graduate from high school and become a rural mail carrier for the U.S. Post Office. That goal was cemented in my mind at a very early age because the family's 1927 Dodge was jacked up on blocks in the barn. Dad couldn't afford three dollars for a state auto license. I recall riding with my father to the county court house, on a snowy day, in a horse-drawn buggy, because we did not have the use of the family automobile. The mail carrier, a Mr. Overholtzer, delivered the mail about noon, to the mailbox down the lane from our farmhouse, in his very own car. I watched with anticipation for his arrival each day. That was the life I wanted.

Shortly after my graduation from high school, Mr. Overholtzer delivered a letter addressed to me. It was dated June 22, 1943 and was from the United States Selective Service. The letter was "greetings" from the Preble County Draft Board and the words that I was anticipating but hoped would never arrive were there.

Dear Wilburn,
Your friends and neighbors have decided that you
should serve your country in the Armed Forces of the
United States of America.

Suddenly, this five foot six, 137-pound, overwhelmed and self-doubting farm boy was a soldier.

Mom and Dad took me to the train station near the county court house. The county official labored to assure the small group of young men how important we were to our country. A local minister gave each of the new inductees a New Testament and repeated the Twenty-third Psalm. I still remember his words on that solemn day, "The Lord is my shepherd. I shall not want. He makes me..."And he sent us off with a prayer for our safety. The tears in Mom's eyes told me that her thoughts mirrored my own—that because of this horrible war we would never see each other again. The train moved southward, and a new life for me was on the horizon.

My memories of those first months are of being homesick—often near tears—in the desert heat of an army base in Texas. Master Sergeant Haggerty, whose job was to make a man out of me, made my life miserable. He succeeded in confirming how totally unimportant I was to this world. Nonetheless, I adjusted and became part of a twelve-man squad whose mission had changed from being part of a homing pigeon company to a signal construction battalion. Digging postholes and learning to climb telephone poles was a change from waiting for a pigeon with a message clipped to its leg to return to its perch. When it was my turn to be the acting platoon drill sergeant, having thirty-six solders respond to my commands of "forward march," "right flank," "to the rear march," and "platoon halt," gave me a new feeling of power and authority.

As a farmer's son, I knew how to work. I was comfortable climbing poles and burying cable and excelled to such a degree that I was promoted to assistant squad leader and became a buck sergeant. Sergeant Haggerty, who remained back in Texas, would have liked seeing this young soldier mature into manhood in Germany. After three years, four months and ten days of military service, I returned to the farm. I was six feet tall, weighed 178 pounds, and was a local hero. Physically I had matured, but there were two events during this period that gave my life new direction and meaning.

First, an older man in my army unit had asked his niece, Ruth Stevens, a high school senior from Chester, West Virginia, to write me. It was a patriotic thing to do at that time. We exchanged letters for almost three years. I eventually found enough boldness to sign them "Love, Willie." Second, our government, through the GI Bill, provided me a tuition-free college education. Going to college was far more enjoyable than the temporary job I had operating a riveting machine at a National Cash Register factory in Dayton, Ohio.

My world was no longer limited to the three miles to town and nine miles to the county seat.

Will as a WWII soldier in June 1943

The Birth of a Merchant

Late 1940s

2

College life at Miami of Ohio was fabulous. No longer were parents or military officers directing my life. Decisions were mine to make and to live by. My academic results were acceptable. My superior achievements in math continued, while my English and composition remained flawed. My first experience outside of my structured life was venturing into Greek fraternity life. With eight other returning servicemen, I chartered the Delta Gamma chapter of Pi Kappa Alpha.

Ruth was in nurse's training at Presbyterian Hospital in Pittsburgh, three hundred miles away. Our blossoming romance was carried on by mail, until the end of my junior year when I found summer work selling water softeners door-to-door in Pittsburgh. Ruth was offered an opportunity to complete the last semester of her education by studying tuberculosis on an Indian reservation in the state of Washington.

We were just going around the next corner in the first stages of our life. We got a marriage license, spent half an hour with a local justice of the peace and were Mr. & Mrs. on a train heading west.

Student Nurse and College Student in 1948

Ruth entered training at an Indian hospital, and I sought employment. Washing dishes at the Poodle Dog Restaurant was the only thing immediately available. I needed a residence and better employment. Unable to find an industrial job, I lowered my farm-boy standards and applied at JC Penney, where there was an opening for a men's hat salesman.

My salary was $185 per month. We decided to enjoy the Great Northwest for six months until I returned to Miami for my senior year. My boss, Jim Weaver, and his wife Peggy, became our good friends. Five months later, a district manager, Mr. Tyler, visited the store. I remember the occasion well. Everybody was as uptight as they had been in the army when a general arrived. Mr. Tyler offered Jim a promotion, but only upon assurance that he had trained someone to take his place. Jim pleaded with me to stay and without telling my bride, I agreed. This was almost like being promoted to buck sergeant in the army. I was now the manager of Penney's work clothes department in one of their eight hundred stores, and I got a $15 raise.

When I thanked my manager for the raise and promotion, he said, "Mr. Morris," (calling me "Mr." meant that what he was about to say was very important), "you only thank people for gifts. You *earned* the raise and promotion." I have benefited from that wise thought throughout my entire career. One year later, I was promoted to manager of their home furnishings department and later the boys' lines were added to my responsibilities.

As a family, we still felt it was the right thing for me to return to college, but strange things happened. A co-worker was called back into the navy to serve in the Korean War, and I took his place. This was the prize first-level management job in the store and I was having the time of my life buying and selling everything that women wear. It was a long way from the farm. My annual salary was $3,600 and a competitor offered me a job managing a dress shop across the street for $7,200. Wow! Of course I would take it. We now had a son, did not own a car, had no rugs on the floor, and cereal and hamburger had to go a long way. We agreed to make the change the first of the next month. For a couple of weeks we were in heaven, just visualizing how we would spend that extra income.

After a week Ruth inquired, "Did you tell Mr. Patterson that you are leaving?"

"No, I'm going to wait for another week. If I tell him now, he might fire me, and we need the pay."

A few days later: "Did you talk to Mr. Patterson?"

"No, it just hasn't worked out. He is always so busy."

"Will, you're not going to tell him, are you?"

A covenant with James Cash Penney had happened. It would survive, at last count, fifty-six years.

JC Penney store #891 Tacoma, Washington in 1950

Time passed, and year after year the people I worked with continued to perform to such an elevated degree that I received recognition. Those ladies in the first store I worked in caused me to be recognized as the top women's fashion manager in our district. Another group resulted in my being promoted from store to district manager, and then the best forty store managers ever assembled caused Will Morris to be become a corporate officer responsible for all stores in one of the company's five regions. We—the five region managers, John, Ken, Bill, Jack and myself—were having fun, being extremely competitive with each other, and getting good corporate results. When our boss, Dave, became president of the company, I was humbled to tears in being asked to replace him. How could this simple farm lad fill the shoes of Bill Marshall, who had once held this position and was visiting the Tacoma store in 1949, the day my oldest son Stan was born? Long retired and living in his hometown in upstate New York, he was the first person I called.

As I traveled the nation on store visits, district and regional meetings, I met many of the "ordinary" performers that made our company great. On most occasions I was introduced to individuals as Mr. Morris, President of Stores. My response was always the same: "Mr. Morris was my dad. My name is Will." To most of the more than one hundred thousand persons in our organization, I was always and only "Will."

Hasan Davis

February 1986

3

My seat was not my selection but an assignment. I was honored to be sitting to the left of Dr. Juanita Krepps at the JC Penney board meetings. A nationally known figure, she chaired the Department of Economics at Duke University, sat on six corporate boards, and served as Secretary of Commerce in President Carter's cabinet. A graduate of Berea College in Berea, Kentucky, she now served the college as a trustee. My acquaintance with Dr. Krepps was brief, but she was pleased to know that I was proud of my Eastern Kentucky heritage and asked if I might be interested in doing some consulting work for Berea College after my retirement. I agreed to meet Berea's president, Dr. John Stephenson.

Berea is indeed unique among institutions of higher learning. Founded in 1855, Berea College was the first interracial and coeducational college in the South, and is consistently ranked as one of the South's top liberal arts colleges. Guided by eight "Great Commitments," Berea provides a high-quality liberal arts education to students of potential high ability but limited financial resources. Berea charges no tuition, awarding the equivalent of a full-tuition scholarship to every student admitted. The college offers rigorous academic programs leading to Bachelor of Arts and Bachelor of Science degrees in twenty-eight fields. All fifteen hundred students are required to work at least ten hours per week. Employed in more than one hundred thirty campus departments, Berea's students are part of an atmosphere of democratic living that emphasizes the dignity of all work. The college has an inclusive Christian character that welcomes "all people of the earth." Students come from all states, and in a typical year there are about sixty international students representing many faiths and cultures. Twenty-five percent of the students represent ethnic minorities.

My consulting efforts during the next two years helped erase an annual $400,000 deficit in the crafts manufacturing and marketing division. That would translate to the annual cost of educating twenty students. Twenty young people, not unlike that farm lad of half a century ago, would see their worlds vastly enlarged. The personal rewards for me were so great that I continued for four more years as an unpaid Assistant to the President, doing development work in Western Pennsylvania. Berea paid for my expenses, which I donated back to the college. My former employer matched this contribution, further bolstering the college's mission.

Part of a course the college offered for seniors was to understand how the college supported itself, since all students were on scholarship. Each member of this class would travel with a development officer. Hasan Davis was assigned to spend a week with me in Pittsburgh. We called on individuals, corporations and foundations that supported the college. Our first appointment was with the director of the Heinz Corporation Foundation. We were invited to view the boardroom of this worldwide corporation. Inside the door Hasan paused; his widened eyes were like pearls contrasting with his black skin. The large oak table was surrounded with ten high-back leather chairs on each side, with an even more imposing chair at each end. He sat in the chair at the head of the table and gazed at the wood-paneled walls and their assortment of large portraits of important people. After a moment of silence, the only sound was his quiet request, "Could I keep this pencil and note pad as a souvenir?"

Richard King Mellon Foundation's Michael Watson, Director of Giving, had declined to support Berea because it was not located in Pennsylvania. He greeted us and was most courteous and attentive. I had informed him that I respected their policy and would not be asking for contributions. The purpose of our visit was to expose a student to the workings of a large foundation.

Michael told us about their founder and his interest in preserving as much of the natural lands of the nation as possible. With a large map on the wall of the conference room he described the colored sections of the map that identified the lands adjacent to national parks that had been purchased and deeded to the government.

Our conversation changed with his suggestion, "Hasan, tell me about you."

"I was born in Indiana but lived in St. Louis as a young child. There were six children. I had one brother and the other four were either step- or half- brothers or sisters. My father, a Baptist lay-minister in the ghetto of St. Louis, deserted my mother. In 1975 she moved us to Atlanta, because it was a place the children might survive. I was diagnosed learning disabled/attention deficit hyperactive at an early age. I've been expelled from every educational unit I have attended. In early grades, being condemned to the cloakroom punished me. In higher grades, I was sentenced to standing in the hall while the class continued, and later was a frequent visitor to the principal's office. I was first arrested at eleven and expelled from alternative school at eighteen."

Filling a pause, Mr. Watson inquired, "Your name, Hasan?"

"I was a puzzled youth. Very much aware that I was dyslexic, couldn't cope with my father deserting his family. During my teen years I embraced my Islamic faith and became Hasan."

He continued, "I knew I was at a crossroads in my life. I earned my GED from the state of Georgia Department of Education. There was a work program at the alternative high school that I attended and through them I first heard about Berea. A contact in Atlanta introduced me to Berea and I was accepted. After three semesters I was expelled because I was not successful at remedial math and English.

"I couldn't go home. That would be the end. So I joined the army for three years. It was a successful experience because I had leadership and direction. I taught a class in martial arts and after one year changed from regular to reserve status and returned to Berea. The admissions office was very cool to my presence. I secured employment as a janitor on campus and each morning for a week presented myself to John Cook, the director of admissions. They gave me a second chance, but only with the understanding that I would be subject to all probations, academic, social and labor. I failed my first class, Freshman Seminar-General Studies. I had failed on making the transition from the strong military leadership to being a self starter."

Michael Watson and I sat in silence waiting—just waiting. Hasan continued, "I was afraid to go back home. I knew that my life would be over if I didn't succeed here. I went to Richmond, twenty-five miles away, and got a job in construction and worked for one year.

"I asked for re-entry to college, was declined, asked again, and was refused. I then sought permission to meet with the committee that made that decision and was granted that courtesy. Before that group started their inquiry I asked for five minutes to state my case.

"I told them that I was very aware that I was a two-time loser and they would be taking a greater risk than I would if they took me back. On the other hand, what validity would it give the college if they gave a student like me three chances to get it right and together we were successful? Wouldn't it describe, beyond all doubt, that the Berea Mission was being fulfilled and everybody would be a winner?

"I was a student again, and the committee granted me a loan to purchase a computer that was programmed to help me with my dyslexic and retention disorder."

Still trying to fathom what we both had heard for the first time, Mr. Watson asked, "How are things going now?"

"I graduate in June. This year I was elected president of the student body and the homecoming king. At graduation I will be the recipient of the V-2 Navy award. The University of Kentucky Law School has accepted me for the fall term."

After some pleasantries Michael Watson asked me to return to his office in a few weeks, and we agreed on a date and time. Upon his recommendation, the foundation agreed to support five students from Western Pennsylvania each year. If they succeeded academically and desired to continue their education, his foundation would contribute a $10,000 annual scholarship toward their advanced degrees. Already, retirement—and I dislike that word—had exposed me to Berea, to President John Stephenson, to Hasan and many other students. Their worlds, like my own, were being expanded far beyond their own "three and nine miles."

And Hasan's world did expand. Today he is an educator, youth advocate and performer. He works nationally with communities exploring creative ways to better value citizens with a history of disenfranchisement. Hasan founded Empowerment Solutions in 1998, following his position as the director of Youth Violence Prevention

Project for the city of Lexington, Kentucky. Now as a consultant/trainer for government, education and community groups, Hasan's primary focus is on issues of youth development, community empowerment and cultural respect.

Hasan uses his experience to create an instant rapport with youth and adults alike. Not many presenters can talk to a room full of Wall Street bankers or an auditorium of maximum-security inmates and receive standing ovations from both. But Hasan has. He is a mediator, a facilitator and trainer in the areas of leadership development, conflict and anger management, community service, cultural competency, entrepreneurship and mentor training. Artistically, Hasan has been recognized as an educator and performer. His artistic work creates an experiential environment for learning. Hasan and his family still reside where he went to college in Berea, Kentucky.

The Accident of Birth

May 1989

4

Native passengers sat along the rail. A thatched roof provided them with shade, while I sat in the hot glaring sun on the opposite side of the deck. Marino stored the provisions he had purchased from the riverfront peddlers beneath the bench where I sat. He departed and returned with a five-gallon glass container of sparkling clear water, a glowing contrast to the brown ice—frozen water from the muddy river—being loaded onto the deck at the rear of the boat.

Startled by the engine blast and black smoke from the exhaust, sea gulls fluttered skyward. The boat vibrated as it backed away from the dirt bank occupied with a mass of native merchants still trying to sell fruit, fresh fish that were coated with mud, bottled drinks and clothing. Even the brown river water was refreshing compared to the filth that was left ashore. Our container of clear water was a source of comfort to me. We moved out into the vast expanse of the river and slowly headed downstream. The commotion of the brazen peddlers hawking their wares passed from sight and mind.

It was quiet. The melody created by the boat interrupting the stillness of the river provided a background for my developing concern. I was completely out of touch with my world and anyone I knew. Marino was a stranger that I had met the previous day on the streets of Manaus. Our transportation was a river version of a local bus moving patiently through the muddy water of the mighty Amazon River. I only knew that I was going someplace into the jungle. My only company was the seven native passengers sitting quietly on the opposite rail staring—their faces frozen without a smile—at me.

Marino's wife, a desk clerk in a small hotel on a dirt street in Manaus, had told me that her husband owned land in the jungle. He would take me there for as many days as I wanted to stay and then return for me. I had met with him, determined a price for transportation, food, and lodging, and agreed to meet him at the dock this morning. I was surprised that we were taking public transportation and that he would buy all of our supplies from the brown-skinned peddlers who swarmed the bank.

My host sat beside me and described our journey in perfect English. His fatherly pride, as he showed me pictures of his two little daughters, eased my fear somewhat. He asked the captain, whom he obviously knew, if I could take the wheel. My new friend put a burlap bag, filled with our supplies, under his head, reclined on a wooden bench, and went to sleep. I drove the "Amazon River Greyhound Bus" through the meandering dirty water and tried to imagine what it would be like to live for five days in the jungle that surrounded this great river.

Four hours passed before our first stop, a store located on one of four rafts that were moored together. This was a river gas station and general store. The store was located in the front, with living quarters in the rear of the largest raft. The merchandise was neatly stacked on shelves and tables. As a retired retailer, I was impressed with the assortment of merchandise available. There were infants' pacifiers, clothing, batteries, packaged food, and even spark plugs. The father was the storekeeper. He was dark, very trim, and except for missing front teeth, a handsome man. The living quarters were in the rear, where the wife and mother sat with her feet in the river, cleaning her aluminum pots in the brown water. Her figure did not match the leanness of her husband. Four small children played nearby. There was no concern for, or protection from, the river. The home was clean and orderly. She acknowledged my presence with a smile. It was obvious to me that both pride and contentment occupied her household.

The four rafts and their contents provided this family with home, a revenue-producing business, and most of their food. The first raft was the store and the family's living quarters. The second raft was a warehouse; its contents included motor oil, soap, canned food, gasoline, straw hats, clothing and unmarked boxes. The third raft was a farmyard and the home for two hogs and a litter of pigs. They were eating white roots, green foliage, and drinking water from the river through a small hole in the floor. Smiling, I thought, pork chops and fish, my favorite meats. The fourth raft, perhaps twenty by forty feet in size, was covered with rich black jungle soil. It was a vegetable garden and its products reflected the abundance of the rich earth, daily rain, and hot sun.

Almost unaware that the boat was on its journey again, I tried to believe what I had just witnessed. It would be a good time to write in my journal but I didn't know how to start. I looked back to confirm that there was a television antenna above the buildings. No electricity and yet a battery-operated TV, and a pool table, and a refrigeration system operated by bottled gas.

As our boat reached its destination and turned directly toward shore, Marino gathered our supplies and placed them on the bow of the boat. The motor idled while we unloaded them on the bank and then the boat returned to its journey. In front of us, up a short hill to drier ground, was a thatched-roof, open-sided structure that would be my residence. A wooden counter, small cast iron stove, metal sink and two hammocks covered by mosquito nets were its only furnishings. I moved in.

Marino explained that my hosts lived next door but were not home. In fact, their home was not home. He cooked my dinner: bread and canned meat, served with cool clear water from the five-gallon jug. My bathroom was a spot in the jungle. Toilet paper, green and soft, grew on the trees. The riverboat on its return trip to Manaus responded to Marino's whistle, and he became a passenger. I was all alone in the Amazon River jungle, somewhere in Brazil.

No one in my world knew that I was sitting on the bank of the world's largest river, deep in a tropical jungle, and not within sight or sound of another human being. I assured myself that God was with me, crawled into the hammock, pulled the mosquito net over me, and fell asleep listening to the stillness of the jungle.

The silence of the morning sunrise was broken by the sound of a small outboard motor. Exhaust smoke veiled the canoe rowboat it powered. A rope connected the boat with a house built on two large partially submerged logs. The home of my hosts—Manuel, Rita, and their four children— was coming home. Their mobile residence was usually parked where Manuel worked in the manioc fields a few miles away. They returned to this location so Rita could cook for whomever Marino brought to his jungle property.

It was May and the seasonal high-water level was at its peak. As far as I could see, the green jungle forest was submerged in slowly moving water. The river had expanded and literally become an ocean, somewhat concealed by the upper portion of the partially submerged trees. I spent my time watching the family and wondered what it must be like to live in this culture and their environment. One evening Manuel took me alligator hunting and we—or rather he—speared a four-foot specimen by blinding it with a flashlight, which he held in his mouth. It was skinned and cooked for dinner. I was not hungry.

On my third day, a boat moving toward me appeared in the distance. I went out in a small motor canoe to meet it. I slowed my engine and then stopped completely as it approached and glided beside me. It was Manuel and Rita's four children. Because their home had been moved back home so their mother could cook my meals, they rowed five miles to their thatch-roofed, open-sided schoolhouse each morning, for their half day of school, and made the five-mile return in early afternoon.

Our language barrier had not prevented me from becoming part of their family. They greeted me with cheerful smiles and extended the international thumbs up sign. They were from six to ten years in age, two boys and two girls, neatly dressed in white knit collarless shirts and navy shorts. They were neat, meticulously clean, and dignified in appearance, more like American children coming home from a parochial school than what one would expect to find deep in the Amazon River country. We exchanged smiles and goodbye waves as they moved on toward their home.

"Accidents of birth" rowing from school

I did not restart my motor, but sat silently watching them row toward their home, the simple wooden structure on the log raft that compensated for the changing water levels in this mighty river. I was very impressed. They were beautiful children. If their minds matched their personalities, they were bright. I was honored to be, although briefly, part of their family.

I could only wonder and imagine what their lives would be like? Based on my brief observation of people who lived here, they would grow into handsome healthy youths with lean tan bodies. They would participate in the typical life of the upper Amazon, where Mother Earth supplies abundant food and basic necessities are easily available. Just like the storekeepers on the rafts, their marriages would produce four children. The women would be excellent mothers and have a magnificent pride of accomplishment in that important role. Their personalities, pride of family, and cheerful spirit would remain, but the lack of activity and the effects of motherhood would change their physical appearance as their waistlines disappeared. The bright smiles would be dimmed as vacancies and darkened teeth would replace the glistening white ones. Time would pass as the sea of water slowly passed, as did their lives. The men's bodies would stay much trimmer and have that dark rugged look, the result of the active life of hunting, fishing and working to provide the needs for the family. Both parents would live in their world and leave it with no opportunity to change it.

It was only natural that I would compare my children and their circumstances to these four. Here I was, at another point in my life's journey with uninhibited time to just sit and think. My pride surfaced as I thought about my four children and their own families. In their world they had achieved success in business, medicine and parenting. Their exposure was different, as was time and location, and most certainly different people affected their lives. I was overcome just thinking about the circumstances of this jungle family's life and my own life and that of my family.

Dave, Sue, Bob, Stan
Celebrating mom's graduation from Chatham

That evening I rowed a hollowed log boat out into the stillness of that quiet expanse of the Amazon. The water was perfectly still and I placed the paddle across the boat, used it for a headrest, and reclined lengthwise. At that moment, as I looked up at a spectacular star-filled sky, it was quiet, motionless and peaceful. Without question, I was alone with my God.

With too much pride and too little humility, I thought about my accomplishments. My rewards as a parent, in my career, and even the privilege of being a traveler and the recipient of today's experience were great. In that quietness I could only admit that others had played a role, larger than mine, for what had been credited to me and given me so much joy and satisfaction. There were many.

Miss Hattie Reed had caused me to understand that there is an answer to every problem, but only if we first understood the problem. My leadership was given credit for major strategic decisions in my forty-year retail career. Her wisdom had provided me with that skill, but I had not selected her to be the teacher of that high school algebra class of eighteen students in the little farm town in Ohio.

Elegant Rae Pugh, the personnel manager, saw something in an insecure young man that led him to change jobs from washing dishes in a restaurant to selling men's hats in her store and growing beyond all expectations in that field. I had nothing to do with her being in my life.

That sweet little high school girl, Ruth Stevens, got my name from her uncle, and as a patriotic gesture, wrote letters to a scared young soldier in Germany. Who could have dreamed that she would become the mother of our four children and the beautiful grandmother of our ten? Knowing her was an accident beyond my control.

Here in the still silence of this great jungle and its majestic river, looking skyward at a million stars, I thought that all the goodness of my life had happened from circumstances over which I had no control. On reflection, my faith assures me that this was God's will for my life, but to me, at that point of time, it was best understood as just an "accident of birth."

Dr. Dave

March 1994

5

I was in my favorite chair reading a book that a friend had suggested would be enjoyable: *Wake Up America*, by Tony Campolo. His example of people desiring to serve rather than be self-serving was interesting. I read:

> *In Pittsburgh, Pennsylvania, there are some young doctors, nurses, practitioners and support staff who have modeled a sacrificial life-style in a profession that has been far too seduced by the allurements of big money. They have established a health center that offers medical services on the basis of people's ability to pay... poor people get the best kind of treatment available in today's world for little or no money. These young people could be on their way to becoming millionaires. Instead they earn a very modest living. The have rejected the ways of the world and have become radical followers of another Great Physician. They are the fruits of a prophetic mentality that seem to be picking up momentum daily.*

I know one of these fine young doctors. I know him well. The story of his journey to this unselfish desire to serve should be told. I will try to write it. On the wall above my computer is a framed article that the *Pittsburgh Press* printed about a transition he had made ten years ago. Even then his story was unique enough to be captured by the press.

My mind drifted back to a rainy stormy morning in the state of Washington. He was at my side, and we were both looking out the dining room window across Phinney Bay. The yacht club, a quarter-mile away on the opposite shore, was barely visible. Turning from the window and walking toward the garage on my way to work I asked, "Any one know where I left my umbrella? It sure is a miserable day."

This little guy's voice boldly proclaimed, "This is the day the Lord hath made: let us rejoice and be glad in it. Psalms 118:24. We learned that in Sunday school."

"OK, Dave I'll try. You have a good day at school." He had just started the first grade.

My youngest son had never been baptized. Our minister, Wilbur Scafe, preferred a ceremony of dedication. "We should dedicate our children to the Lord," he said. "They can decide for themselves at an age of accountability." Over the years, when Dave was so logically reaching decisions, I have often recalled Rev. Scafe's words, "May this David reach the greatness of the Psalmist, King David." And there was my David, quoting words from King David's psalms to encourage his father's entrance into a stormy morning.

Another late afternoon, while a simple piano melody filled the room, I heard him say, "Mom, what difference does it make?" His mother simply couldn't understand why he insisted on practicing his piano lessons before removing that broad-shouldered, often soiled, football uniform.

"At least you can put the helmet under the bench," she replied.

Mom never gave him evidence that the soiled uniform affected the quality of his music. There was never an argument. He only expressed logic—most often sound logic—backed by reasons or convictions.

His logic was demonstrated at an early age on a walk to the grocery store when we lived in Pasadena, California.

"Dad, where did you and Mom go last night?"

"Out to dinner and to a movie."

"What show did you see?"

"A comedy called, 'What Did You Do In The War Daddy?'"

"Oh."

We were both barefoot just walking a couple blocks to the grocery store. As tenderly as possible our path moved from one shady spot to the next and then to the shade of a tree to cool the burning soles of our feet. He looked up at me and asked, "Dad, were you in a war?"

"Sure."

"Were you a soldier?"

"Yeah."

"What did you do in the war, Daddy?"

"Nothing much. We had better get going. Your mother needs that milk for something. If we don't hurry we'll have another war."

Moving step for step beside me he looked up and asked, "Where were you in the war?"

"Germany." I moved faster from one point of shade to the next, more to discourage the conversation than to evade the hot concrete.

"Did you fly a plane?"

"No o o o o."

"Did you drive a tank?"

My hasty and, hopefully final "no" followed.

"Dad, did you have a gun? Did you shoot a gun?"

"Yes, Dave, I shot a gun lots of times."

"Really! Did you kill any Germans?" His voice expressed hope and enthusiasm until my disappointing reply caused total silence.

With milk in hand we returned home. Dave followed a

few steps behind until the green soft grass in our yard cooled our tender feet. Again, looking up, his logic verified, he confirmed his conclusion, the decision he had made, with a question for me.

"Dad, you really didn't do much in the war did you?"

His judgment required no reply on my part.

Dave's two brothers, three and five years older, required disciplined daily medication. The answer to his question, "If they take medicine why don't they get well?" always left him with a very puzzled look on his face.

Dave's two brothers and his sister attended college and everyone except Dave assumed that he would do likewise. He and I would do battle, friendly but determined battle, for at least three years over this issue. His weapon was his belief that his future was his responsibility. My sword was a definition of leadership as the ability to cause people to act as you want, with them convinced that it was their idea.

The first round lasted fifteen months. "Dad, I've been in school for twelve years and during that time we've moved eight times. I'm tired. I'd just like to go back out West and get a job and decide what I want to do."

"Dave, that's a big risk. If you do that you may never go to college and you'll never know what you have missed."

"You didn't go to college after high school."

"That was different. I didn't have a choice. The draft board made that decision for me."

"You've told me many times that you were glad you were in the army before college. I just want to do something first. You didn't have a choice but I do and I just don't want to go to college now."

He had the upper hand. We never argued and neither of us ever lost our cool. This was a debate and he had made his point. My respect for him almost caused me to surrender. I only retreated, not in defeat but to try another approach, at another time.

Days, weeks, several months passed. The seriousness of the conversations about college was disguised by lightheartedness. I teased him about college being too tough for him to maintain his high grade point average. He responded by describing how he would spend his own earnings.

"Dave, if you don't go to school next year you run the risk of becoming involved and developing a life without the benefits of a higher education. It could be the best life ever but you would never know. What if you went to college one year and then made that decision? You would always have the college experience as your own basis for comparison."

The fact that he did not interrupt and did not reply pleased me. His first year at the university was a pleasant one, certainly for his parents. His grades were good, and he made new friends. I asked him to return the second year, and he reluctantly did, but only after my promise not to make another request. I made no further demands, and he did not return after his sophomore year. He went to California, and had two jobs. He worked in a bicycle shop in the evenings and on weekends, which paid for his room and board. The wages he earned working in a warehouse were savings.

When the fall college term started he was at the Oregon/California border with a mongrel dog that had belonged to his brother. Two hundred and twelve miles of the John Muir Trail flowed through the mountains southward. With a tent, backpack, camping gear and his dog, he wandered its length before returning to school in February.

His reply to my inquiry, "Have you determined a major?" always got the same answer.

"Dad, I just don't have the slightest idea. I know you are entitled to more for your investment but I just don't know." The fraternity environment appealed to him. His contribution helped his fraternity achieve the best grade point average.

Dr. Kohler, head of the accounting department, was the faculty advisor for the fraternity. This association led to accounting classes and to a business major. Interest in accounting led to serving his fraternity as treasurer. In his senior year he was their president.

Graduation was midterm. He came home to study for his CPA exams. During this time he took an Emergency Medical Technician course at a local community college, volunteered for ambulance duty three nights a week, and worked at a local restaurant as a waiter.

It was good to have him home and we continued our enjoyable discussions and debates on a multitude of subjects. We even agreed politically. I specifically recall his thoughts one evening as he prepared to leave for his midnight to daybreak ambulance duty. His voice was concerned. "Oh, I hope there are no serious accidents tonight. But if there are, I hope they are in our territory." Thoughtfully and silently, he walked out the front door.

"Dad, I've been thinking, would being a CPA be that important?" Restlessness caused the ambulance riding, studying for the exam, and job at the restaurant to be replaced by signing on to a wheat harvest crew. From Oklahoma to southern Canada, he followed the harvest. His classroom was a powered combine that reaped wide swathes of grain from the time the morning dew disappeared until it reappeared, sometimes in the wee hours before daybreak. His residence was a mobile bunkhouse, his meals came from the mobile kitchen, and recreation was the local taverns that these combine cowboys frequented when grain was not ripe or weather not suited for harvest. Rumor had it that the ranch owners put their daughters under lock and key when the combine cowboys came through.

To the reporter who interviewed him for the *Pittsburgh Press* story he said, "After going around the edge of a field once too often I decided I was bored and life was passing me by." With the assistance of the university, he entered a training program with Bethlehem Steel.

Overnight, he became an expert in the steel industry, from the financial perspective. Without question he was identified as a young talent with a purpose and on a fast track. I was pleased when he related, "I'm flying to Chicago next week on the corporate jet." Things were going great for him. He had worked for eighteen months, had good performance reviews, two generous raises, and was home for a weekend visit.

"Dad, I've been thinking." I had learned that when Dave says, "I've been thinking," you know something big is about to happen. He has been thinking, and he has been thinking seriously for a long time, and his mind is set. What will it be? "I just can't crunch numbers for the rest of my life. How would you feel if I went back to school?"

After a short moment's reflection, my thoughtful response was, "I've spent half my life trying to get you through college and now you won't stop. Tell me about it."

"I want to go into medicine."

"Dave, that's great! Guess I'll have to give up on you becoming an attorney, and your mom will never have her minister."

"Dad, be serious. It will take seven years before I earn a living. Would you be willing to help financially? I have no right to ask. You have already done so much."

"Doctor David W. Morris, be my guest."

My son, Doctor Dave! I couldn't believe it. The kid that didn't want to go to college, the kid that hiked the John

Muir trail, the kid that drove a wheat combine across the great wheat fields of the Midwest, the kid that became an accountant, the kid that rode on the corporate jet. Yes, my youngest kid! He wanted to be a doctor. Seven medical schools accepted him. His age, background, experiences, and academic performance impressed them. He was a new person, neither excited nor unexcited about his new life and surroundings, just content and satisfied.

After seven more years of study, marriage to a classmate, Karen, and the birth of their first child, at thirty-three he was ready to start his career. An enormous number of opportunities: private practice, teaching, and new innovative medicine, were available. He chose to work in a small hospital in a blue-collar area of Pittsburgh because, he said, "I want to be a doctor and deal with patients."

Dr. Reed, one of his favorite faculty members at the University of Pittsburgh Medical School, one year later asked him to be on the faculty of the residents' program at Shadyside Hospital. It would involve teaching, dealing with patients and working with young doctors. His respect for Dr. Reed, the security of the job, and the opportunity to be a patients' doctor made the offer tempting. He was thinking again: "I'm too young and don't have enough experience to direct those young residents. It wouldn't be right."

Dr. Hall, director of the East Liberty Family Health Care Center, the group described in Tony Campolo's book, made Dave an offer he couldn't refuse: be part of one of the city's finest family care medical facilities. "Care for people who are sick. If patients can't come to the clinic we go to their homes. If they can't pay, or have no insurance, there is no charge for what we do. We are here to give the best medical care possible because people need it. The doctor's income? That is determined by what funds we receive."

Shadyside Hospital and Dr. Reed were disappointed when Dave declined their offer. It was hard for them to understand, and they listened with interest to his explanation. Their response turned from disappointment to admiration for the wheat harvester, accountant, ambulance rider and trail hiker, turned doctor. Shadyside Hospital underwrote one half of the salary they had offered him as a guarantee as long as he was associated with East Liberty Family Health Center.

The printed announcement of Dave's arrival at the Health Care Center read:

Welcome Dr. Morris

David W. Morris, M.D., family practice physician, joined ELFHCC as a full-time physician April 1, 1993. Before joining us Dr. Morris was on the staff of Forbes Metropolitan Hospital Family Practice Department in Wilkinsburg.

Dave and his wife, Karen are the parents of two children, Thad age 2 1/2 years and Hanna age 10 months. We are very pleased and blessed to welcome Dr. Morris and his family to our family at East Liberty Health Care Center.

The announcement concluded: "God is Good."

I looked up from my computer at a picture of Dave the medical student, studying. Had I been able to tell, in words, the story of Doctor Dave? Certainly not. The story of Doctor Dave is just beginning.

Tourist or Traveler

September 1989

6

The sun had been absent for three days. Across the street the people in their colorless dress, just like the gray climate, walked, looking neither ahead, nor right, nor left, seemingly without purpose or destination. A trolley appeared, reached the end of the line, and slowly turned in preparation for its return trip. I joined the people waiting to board. At each stop, riders, without expression or expectation, boarded and departed. They sat or stood silently. I could only imagine that their faces and actions reflected the hope of most people in this socialist country.

The view abruptly changed as we passed formidable government buildings with marble courtyards, impressive statues, and green manicured lawns. The streetcar stopped in front of a very modern Sheraton Hotel. Tourists dominated the area in front. To the Sofia residents, these visitors' dress was very foreign, as were the obvious cameras and the colorful shopping bags. These guests had not arrived, nor would they depart, on a dingy trolley. The large white air-conditioned bus with the government tourist insignia boldly painted on each side waited for them. A well-trained, very professional travel guide, representing the tourist industry and the communist government, would explain to these tourists the merits and beauty of this Bulgarian capital.

On this morning, for me, the dining room of the Sheraton was passage into another world. The courteous waitress, immaculately dressed and speaking perfect English, placed my breakfast in front of me. The white linen tablecloth supported the silver eating utensils, colored napkin and silver-trimmed china. The golden yolks of two eggs placed perfectly in the center of the plate stared at me. The aroma of rye toast and crisp bacon energized my appetite. It had been seven months since I had tasted bacon. It was a stark contrast to my first meal in this country three days earlier, when I had walked from the train station, found a bench beneath a tree, ignited my camp stove, heated water for instant coffee and enjoyed a piece of hard bread from my pack.

After my delightful breakfast, I paused to listen to the conversation of three tourists, obviously American, on the steps outside the hotel. Observing that my dress was not like theirs, that I carried no camera or shopping bag, they responded to my "Good Morning," with surprise. Nonetheless they welcomed my participation. They were part of a two-week tour and were staying at this Sheraton hotel. We compared experiences. They had seen the modern subway in Hungary but I had seen the marble platforms of the subway in Leningrad. They described the fine restaurants in Sofia while I unsuccessfully tried to challenge their view of this country by telling them about the poor and inadequate food supply in the stores where residents bought their food.

Our conversation became a duel. I halted the sparring by asking, "Have you been to Romania?"

Their voices were in spirited unison, "We just finished our tour yesterday." Assuming I had not been there, they bombarded me with the excitement of their experience. Immediately, I became the audience, and they were the speakers, just like any friend, armed with slides and a projector, telling you about travel to a place you have never seen.

"Our guide was unsurpassed in his fluent English and knowledge of history. We were amazed at Romania's beauty and quality. The museums and the beautiful government buildings were magnificent. The subway system was superior to any in the U.S." They had enjoyed what they had learned and their enthusiasm caused one to interrupt another in order to tell her version of the experience. I wanted to tell them about the Romania that I had seen, but decided not to. It would serve no purpose. We had been to the same country but they had seen what the tourist saw and I had witnessed Romania through the eyes of a very fortunate traveler. As I returned to the dingy streetcar and rode back to the end of the line, I could only compare what I envisioned their experience had been with my own.

I had learned that the most-needed commodity for Romania was hard currency from the U.S., U.K., and Germany. The most effective way for the government to acquire it is through a controlled, sophisticated tourist industry—and their target customer is any affluent foreigner. These tourists lodge in the best of hotels and dine in elegant restaurants, both of which only accept U.S. dollars or other hard currency. They only reside and dine with other affluent tourists and never interface with the country's residents—with the exception of trained tourist personnel. Their transportation is large white air-conditioned busses that are detested by the masses that reside in this country. The sights they see are those that the government wants to show them. Its goal is to have them impressed with what they see and return to their homelands assured that people in Romania are happily living under a communist government.

My little trolley rolled on but I was unaware of its location as I was lost in thought about my visit to Bucharest. Traveling Romania or any Third World or underprivileged countries we often use the term, "quality of life" to describe the living conditions of the average citizen. The value of local currency is a sure indication of quality of life. In my journals I had recorded: "Poland, July 1, 1989, Government exchange rate 819 zlotys for $1. On the street peddlers offer 6000 zlotys for $1. Leningrad, July 18, 1989. At the government bank I exchanged $10 for five rubles. In the men's room I bought 100 for $10. Budapest, September 15, 1989. The official exchange rate was 59 forints for $1. I paid a moneychanger $10 for 1,000 forints.

Although openly practiced, it was illegal to buy black market money. After months of travel, my caution had turned to confidence and my confidence to boldness. The excitement of being a criminal—not to mention the economic advantage—prompted me to buy black market currency in every country where the practice flourished. I had become addicted to the thrill. But Romania would be different.

Other travelers had warned me, "Don't exchange for black market money." The U.S. Consulates in both Czechoslovakia and Hungry advised me to stay out of Romania, but sensing that I was determined to go, made sure that I understood that if I was caught buying local currency from other than official sources, I would end up in jail. There was a great likelihood, I was warned, that anyone who approached you and talked about money was probably a government agent trying to trap you. I even bought a carton of Kent cigarettes. My "Travel Guide" said they were the most valuable trading commodity in the country. Not just cigarettes, but Kents. Success in Romania would surely be the peak of my achievements.

My first class train ticket, purchased in Budapest for the 693-kilometer ride to Bucharest, cost the equivalent of five dollars. A real bargain! Ten miles inside the Romanian border the train stopped at the first small town. Here the economics changed drastically. Soldiers, armed with machine guns, stood at each train door as the Hungarian crew departed. Uniformed Romanian personnel took command. The first order of business was to stamp my passport at a charge of $20 per day for a three-day visit. The train was scheduled to enter the country just prior to midnight and wait until after midnight on the return trip. My three-day visa, because of their programmed train schedule, cost $100. This was the first indication of their worthless money. Adding insult to injury, they devalued my money fifty percent so it would cost me $200 just to stay in their pilfering country for three days. Remember that $5 train ticket bargain.

A large, leathery-looking policeman demanded the next intrusion into my financial resources. He checked my newly acquired and expensive visa and advised me that the government required that I exchange $140 for Romanian currency for each of the five days specified on my visa to pay for food and lodging. He could not understand English when I suggested that I would only be there three days. We argued until I gave him $700. He handed me 6,000 Romanian lei, an exchange rate of nine lei for one dollar— less, of course, a commission of 300 lei. The train moved away from the station. I stretched out across the three seats in the compartment to sleep. The first fifteen miles of travel in Romania had cost me $905, and I needed to sleep. A uniformed official shook me with his boot and advised me that if I wanted to sleep I would have to buy a ticket for the sleeping coach. He waited for his bribe. I handed him a pack of Kents and spent the night sleeping across the three seats.

Shortly after dawn, tired and sleepy, I left the train and entered the cold, sterile Bucharest station. A smiling, flamboyantly-dressed, and suspiciously helpful man welcomed me to his country. He offered to get me a taxi, find me a hotel and, almost as an afterthought, "If you need money I can give you 1,500 lei for $10." Confident that he was an agent trying to trap me I moved on into the street with my wealth of 6,000 lei, that the government had forced me to pay $700 for. It would have cost me $40 "on the street." Now I understood why they arrested you for buying their worthless money. "What the hell," I thought. "Maybe I'll do it just to spite them."

After three days of wandering and wondering, being aware of suspicious stares, I was ready to get out of the country and see Belgrade. Without question I had been followed, watched and suspected. It would be a relief to cross the border. At lunch, at a prominent hotel near the U.S. Embassy, I started to ask the waiter to sell me money but got cold feet and backed down. My pocket still bulged with money I had not been able to spend. There was nothing of value to buy. Anything of value that a visitor would buy required U.S. dollars, German marks, or English pounds.

That night I went to a hotel near the station to celebrate dinner before my train departed. A table on the patio had a reserved sign, in English. A young waiter, speaking perfect English, informed me that the table was reserved for hotel guests. I handed him a pack of Kents, which I would no longer need, and he politely removed the sign.

It was a fine dinner, one only a tourist could afford. The waiter was friendly and talked freely except for questions about government. The pack of Kents had set the stage. As a waiter in a tourist hotel, he was allowed to talk to foreigners without suspicion. He talked with pride and respect about his Turkish wife and their year-old son. He was a proud husband and father and hoped that some day his life would be better. In a hushed tone, he said he would like to go to Turkey to live but that was not possible.

My dinner, which took more than an hour, consisted of the most expensive items on the menu. There was wine in a chilled glass, a small thin steak, potatoes, vegetable, and bread, then cake for dessert, and coffee. My check was 200 lei, $22 worth of the money I bought on the train. On the street it would be $1.30.

I had evil thoughts again. Maybe it was my disgust for this country. In my weakness I wanted to strike back by breaking their law and getting away with it. The waiter returned to my table and with all the nerve at my command I asked, "Can I pay with American money?"

"Sure," without hesitation.

Regretting that I had asked I followed with, "How much change will you give me if I pay with a $10 bill?"

Sure that secret police were watching me, I tried to remain calm. Knowing that my $10 was still in my money belt helped. As yet, no transaction had taken place. He returned, leaned over my shoulder and whispered, "It's OK. I give you 1,000 lei for ten dollar. You pay for dinner."

I don't remember whether I wanted to call it off or felt bullish enough to bargain. I did however ask him to bring me 800 lei in change and said I would leave the $10 under the napkin for him to retrieve after I left. He agreed.

He returned, after what seemed like forever, placed the illegal money beside my dinner plate, and left. I sat at the table trying to decide whether I was a hero or a fool. Still safe from arrest, I moved back from the table, went to the men's room, took a ten-dollar bill from my money belt, and returned to my chair. I had a great desire to look around for agents, but I wanted to appear calm.

My moist, nervous hand picked up the lei and put it in the pocket of my jeans. Sliding the $10 bill under the napkin was the point of no return for me. Sitting silently, I waited, sure that an authoritative hand would touch my shoulder, but nothing happened. Making sure the napkin covered the money and with guarded caution, I left the dining area and began my walk through the lobby.

I don't remember his name, but I'll never forget the voice that broke the silence as I hurriedly walked across the hotel lobby, confident that I had successfully broken the law. It was my waiter. "I got problem, come with me." Panic and fear gripped me. How could I have been so stupid? The abundance of illegal currency that bulged from my pocket quickly changed from an asset to a liability. The front-page story of my hometown newspaper flashed across my mind. The headlines would read: "Morris Jailed in Bucharest, Romania: Economic Crimes, Exchange of Illegal Money." He escorted me across the hotel lobby where a government agent would certainly interrogate me, and I had no defense. I could only think, "How could a grown man be so stupid?" Why had I ignored all the signals that said don't do it?

There were just the two of us in this small storage room. He was very nervous. Maybe he was in trouble too; maybe he would be my cellmate. Then he calmed and said, "Let me explain." In a slow deliberate manner he told me he had paid for my dinner with his own money because he wanted the ten dollars to buy a very special gift for his wife and son in the duty-free shop off the hotel lobby. Only foreigners with a passport could make a purchase. Expressing love and devotion for his wife and son, he handed me the ten-dollar bill and described the gift he wanted me to purchase for him.

There was no hesitation; he knew what he wanted. He described it to me and waited at the entrance while I went into the shop and made the purchase. The item cost $2.50 so I bought four, returned to where he waited and handed the bag to him. He was ever so grateful, thanked me, and walked away with his prize and a happy smile.

All my anxiety about being a convict, jailed in a Romanian prison, had been unnecessary. The frame of this young man's life had revealed what I could not fathom. His wife and son would have a gift that they could only have dreamed of. As I walked toward the train station I momentarily forgot about the night's train ride. I would rather have been in the home of that young waiter and witness him sharing this important gift, which never had been available in their world. Perhaps they would save one of the small bright blue aluminum bags of Planters Peanuts until their year-old son was old enough to hear and understand the story about the stranger who had come into their life.[1]

That stranger was a *traveler* not a *tourist*.

[1] On December 16, 1989, Romanian security forces cracked down on tens of thousands of citizens in Timisoara. As many as two thousand were killed. On December 21, 1989, the demonstrations spread to Bucharest. Ceausescu was shouted down during a public speech. On December 25, 1989, Ceausescu and his wife were captured, tried for crimes against the state, and executed. Heavy casualties occurred at the hotel where I had had dinner the day that Ihad bought the peanuts, just three months earlier.

Flight Training

June 1986

7

I practiced two and one half-hours to build up my confidence for a longer trip. At several local airports I practiced landings, primarily to get comfortable with talking to air traffic control and the control towers. The plane that I used, the one I learned to fly in, developed some mechanical problems so the flight school checked me out in a new Cessna 172 with only fifty hours on it. Its avionics were much more sophisticated than my training plane.

I departed Sunday at 5:00 P.M. intending to fly northeast. But the flight service station at Allegheny Airport, in Pittsburgh, advised me that weather would not permit a visual flight, and I was a long way from being instrument-rated. The weather looked good to the southwest, so I headed for Huntington, West Virginia, and maybe Cincinnati. The new aircraft was equipped with a transponder (radar), so for the first time I asked air traffic control for "flight following." They would keep track of me on radar and stay in radio contact, a good security blanket.

Except for going around a couple of billowing white cumulus clouds that were too frightening to fly through, I followed a radio vector to Parkersburg and then on to Huntington. Weather service at the airport advised me that even though there were numerous clouds and the possibility of rain showers, it was perfectly safe for a conservative, novice, and grandfatherly pilot to fly to Cincinnati.

Airborne again and playing with the new avionics, I discovered how to tell the distance to the next control point. Fifty miles from the airport I called the tower and proudly identified myself, "Cessna 0442, inbound fifty miles east."

The controller asked me to turn five degrees to the right and runway 27L came into view. I cautiously and courageously settled toward it.

"Cessna 0442, an inbound DC 9 will be landing on 27R. Acknowledge when you have it in sight."

As proudly and as professionally as I could I uttered, "Cessna 0442 has DC 9 at nine o'clock."

We glided to the runways side by side. The huge jet made a much smoother landing than the Cessna and the pilot's palms were probably less sweaty. Waiting for permission to taxi to the ramp, I counted twelve commercial aircraft departing, landing, or waiting. My heart pounded against my chest wall: all those big guys and little me. It was a fabulous first leg, but I was ready to lay my head on a pillow at the Red Roof Inn.

There was sun the next morning but it would surely rain. For the first time in my flying career, I filed a Visual Flight Plan, from Cincinnati south to London, Kentucky. There was a flight service station at the London airport where I could get weather before heading east over the mountains.

Airborne at about twenty-five hundred feet, I approached a rain cloud. Respecting its force I flew around it. It reminded me of the shower in my bathroom, forcefully spraying water onto a confined area. Another first for the novice pilot.

Moments later another cloud appeared and with my growing confidence I bravely penetrated it. Moving at more than one hundred knots into a forceful cloudburst produced the sound and rapidity of a machine gun. It ceased just as quickly as it started, and quiet prevailed.

After passing the Lexington airport, with clear weather ahead, I followed the freeway south until I sighted the Berea College campus. It was fun to circle the town and campus and see from the air what I had seen on my trip to visit President Stephenson three weeks earlier. I wondered if he could imagine that Will was flying over his campus.

Using the highway as a guide, I flew toward London as the sky before me was turning very dark. Still in a cautious, conservative mindset, I was confident knowing that the two gas tanks were full, the weather behind me was clear, and I knew how to contact the controller. In fact, the radio was still set on his frequency. Weather personnel at the London airport easily convinced me that this was the end of my flying for today, so I found a Ramada Inn and called it a short second day.

This was my first time in London, and it brought back family memories. My mother had attended school in a one-room school at the head of Elk Creek in Clay County, Kentucky for eight years, and then became the teacher. During the summer months, she traveled to London and attended normal school to acquire her certification to continue to teach. I was comfortable spending time here and wanted to see the downtown area. The force of the rain hitting the ground caused the dirt to bounce upward. My uniform for the walk to town was swimming trunks, a short-sleeved shirt, and bare feet.

Completely soaked, I found shelter in a pool hall and played an expensive—twenty-five cents—game of pool. The short cut across a freshly-cut hay field back to the motel was a mistake, as the soles of my bare feet were evidence. An old farmer in a beat up pickup truck loaded with peaches came by. I bought five beautiful peaches from him for one buck, and that was my dinner.

Morning found the weather still socked in. I had to wait until eleven for it to clear, which gave me time to take inventory of my predicament. Charlotte, N.C., my next stop, was three hours southeast across the Smoky Mountains. Their highest elevation was forty-seven hundred feet. The flight weather station advised me that the base of the cloud cover was four thousand feet and the clouds topped out at eight thousand. I couldn't fly under four thousand and risk slapping a mountain, so I would have to find a way to go over the top. Just like Charles Lindbergh did when he lifted his plane from the runway on Long Island for his trip into the unknown and perhaps Paris, I left the asphalt for my unknown and perhaps Charlotte.

The clouds were beautiful, puffy, cumulus types but so high I didn't know if I could get above them without going through them, and for a non-instrument-rated pilot that was too risky. After flying about forty miles, I kept wondering when to start climbing and frankly considered turning back. An opening, looking like a valley, lay ahead and I raised the nose and started climbing through the valley in the sky. Because there was no point of reference to give me a feeling of speed, it appeared that I was suspended in space. I was moving ever-so-slowly in a wonder world. The valley closed in front of me, but a glimmer of sunlight suggested there might be an opening. I turned to face it, followed another little valley up into the brilliant sunlight and on top. After staying at that level for another hour and feeling secure that I had crossed the mountains, I dropped below the now-broken cloud cover.

With a mixture of humility and pride I turned the radio frequency to Charlotte and announced, "Charlotte control, this is Cessna 0442 seventy-two miles on 276 inbound for landing. Could I have flight following?"

The reply made me feel very professional: "Cessna 0442 squawk 2742 (radar identification). Visibility fifteen miles, clear. Advise ten miles out."

After refueling, I asked tower for departure to Myrtle Beach. Seven US Airways jets were holding for clearance onto the runway. Probably just to get me out of the way a sweet tower voice let me intercept the runway one thousand yards ahead of the waiting jets and depart with the understanding that at five hundred feet I would make a sharp turn to the left at a heading of 350. Pride swelled inside as I imagined the conversation in the cockpits as my little ole putt-putt got departure preference.

At the Pittsburgh airport where I learned to fly, the runway is twelve hundred feet above sea level. The standard approach to a landing strip is eight hundred feet above the runway. It became routine, for me, to drop down and level off when the altimeter reached two thousand feet. The airport at Myrtle Beach is just off the Atlantic beach. The voice in my headset said, "Cessna 0422 cleared to land runway 05." I descended at my normal rate and found myself midway over the runway much too high to land.

Embarrassing as it was I advised the tower that I would do a go-around. On the second try I did the same thing and overshot the runway. After two go-arounds, I got it on the ground. My professionalism disappeared.

Heavy thunderstorms prevented my early departure the next morning. When the last one blasted through, I left for Greensboro. I had been spending lots of time in the air and not practicing the other parts of flying. I spent the day locating eight different county uncontrolled airports. I practiced identifying my presence, getting into traffic patterns, and doing touch-and-goes. It was fun to land at these out-of-place airports, kick tires, have coffee, and chat with the other "Will Morrises" that hang around airports.

The Greensboro radar departure control monitored me to Mercer County Airport in Bluefield, West Virginia. It was a beautiful flight. I could not see the airport behind the last hill, but I knew it would be there. The runway rose to meet the wheels and there was not a sound or bounce. My practice was paying off. Weather looked good for the next leg to Roanoke and then Manassas, Virginia. My stop in Roanoke caused me to remember my first flight in a small plane, when I needed to get from San Francisco to Greenbriar, West Virginia for a three-hour meeting. I flew commercial from San Francisco to Roanoke, and then hired a private pilot to fly me to Greenbriar. It was snowing as we crossed the mountains and dropped into the small airport at the hotel. I made a pledge that if I got out of the plane alive I would never be guilty of flying in a small plane again.

I stopped at Manassas, a small airport south of the Washington, D.C. airspace. I wanted to get my breath before flying, or attempting to fly, through that complicated air space. Each airport—Washington National, Baltimore/Washington International, Dulles International, Andrews Air Force and six small airports—has its own towers. Washington Air Traffic Control guides you to the airport and then turns you over to the tower. The attendant at Flight Service told me that they would not answer my request for clearance because they didn't want me in their air space, so I decided to fly around it to Lancaster, PA. But once airborne I contacted Dulles departure frequency; they gave me a "squawk" (transponder setting) and guided me through.

On a roll and feeling great, I went from Lancaster, to Reading, to Wilkes Barre, to Poughkeepise, NY, to Bridgeport, Conn., with lunch and coffee breaks, topping off gas and having fun. The controller chewed me out for failing to follow the tower's instructions and flying over a noise abatement residential area at Bridgeport. From there I flew down the Long Island Sound about five hundred feet above the water and below the traffic control altitude. It was a beautiful sunny afternoon and I enjoyed watching the pleasure craft playing in the water. After a short stop at East Hampton, I flew out past Montouk Point and back to McArthur Airport and camped at a Holiday Inn nearby. On the day I had planned to go back to Pittsburgh, I was at the eastern end of Long Island and on the edge of the busiest air space in the world. International flights come in to JFK, Newark is busy with continental and regional flights, and Tetoboro is the hub of private corporate aircraft. I could sneak south or north and go around it, or I could file a flight plan and attempt to go through it. I chose the latter, and after a thirty-five minute wait at the end of the runway, clearance control finally accepted my little puddle jumper into the world of commercial aircraft. From Long Island to the Hudson River I was switched to three different controllers, all of whom talked a mile a minute with that hard-to-understand New York accent. They directed me north to the George Washington Bridge. Over my shoulder I could see Manhattan sitting beside the lazy Hudson. An unusually friendly controller asked if I was doing OK, and after assuring him I was, I asked if I could fly down the Hudson.

"Sure, if you drop down to five hundred feet below the controlled air space."

Only the current of the river beneath me was moving slower than the busy world of aircraft above me, the activity of the most unbelievable city in the world to my left, and the hundreds of cars racing along the highways on both sides of the river. Forward to my left was the incredible spectacle of the World Trade Center Towers of Lower Manhattan and directly ahead was the Lady with the Torch. I moved to my left to get a better look and remembered seeing her on my return from Europe aboard a troop ship in 1945. I could even hear the band aboard the welcoming boat that came to greet us as we returned from the war.

I returned to the controller, thanked him, and told him I would just stay at this level and fly visual to Pittsburgh. I don't know what his day was like, but he had made my day. I used the next two hours flying home to recollect my flying career to date. Pride caused me to acknowledge that I had matured from a student to a pilot—that is, until the airport tower cleared me to land at Allegheny Airport and I couldn't find it. After I asked for his help, the controller kindly directed me to the runway and, knowing that I was either excited or tired, asked me if I had the runway numbers in sight.

When I had left home four days earlier, I had anticipated an adventure but never imagined how exciting it would be. I felt cautious but comfortable with the equipment and how to use it. One thing was for sure: I was going to study for my instrument rating so I could fly in weather.

Will and co-pilot Ruth enjoy an afternoon flight. Will learned to fly and earned his pilot license at age 60.

Smooth Gin Martini

April 1989

8

For half an hour I sat silently and enjoyed both the taste and the resulting relaxation of the prized blend of vermouth and gin. The ice cubes clinked against the glass as my finger rotated its final time. There was just one more taste. "Mmmm, that sure is good."

Three small cubes of ice, like three eyes, stared upward as I reflected on my journey to this table and the warmth and comfort of this soothing drink. My poor body was tired and had reason to be; an afternoon flight from my home to JFK, an evening flight to Miami, a midnight departure on Pan Am for Rio, very little sleep, a long wait in the aisle for the bathroom, trying to understand the Portuguese dialogue of a Brazilian movie, and then being awakened for a breakfast I didn't want after my exhaustion had finally turned to sleep.

The bright morning sun in Rio should have been a tonic but my soul was too tired to respond. The four-hour wait for the flight to Santiago did little to rekindle my spirit. I had little taste for the vast, duty free shopping complex that opposed my concept of a foreign country. Finally I was airborne again, bound for Santiago and trying to stay awake long enough to be concerned with customs, currency, lodging and language.

Somehow these issues were all resolved, and my first foreign purchase was a one-dollar bus ticket that entitled me to a dusty twenty-mile bus ride from the airport to the center of the city. A twelve-block walk, carrying my heavy luggage along a dusty cobblestone street to a small hotel, completed the exhaustion that had started twenty-four hours earlier in Pittsburgh.

A shower and the miracle of a bed brought welcomed rest. The body that demanded sleep wrestled with a curious mind that wanted adventure. One was saying, "Go to sleep," while the other was saying, "OK, let's see what's out there." The conflict continued and replaced my needed nap.

Feeling very much an alien and with heavy feet I wandered into Spanish Santiago. Palm trees, dirty cobblestone streets, dark complexions, and shiny black hair. Completely out of context with what I was adjusting to appeared a bright neon sign with Chinese characters—a Chinese restaurant. Tired, confused as to who I was or where I was, I opened the door and entered the comfort of a restaurant not unlike one near my home in Pittsburgh. For a moment I was not a stranger. Greeted with a gracious bow and a warm welcoming, smile, I was escorted to a table. The patrons were all native and the employees were Chinese. Four people at an adjoining table looked toward me, acknowledging that I was unfamiliar in their surroundings. Still the alien, I was the strange one.

My waiter, slight in stature, handed me a menu. He retreated slightly, bowed, smiled and spoke in Spanish. Pointing to myself and looking into his face I explained, "American. Speak English?"

The expression of disappointment on his face foretold the negative movement of his head and the soft, "So-w-rry, no Ing-lis." An oriental menu printed in Spanish and a waiter who couldn't understand my language were overwhelming obstacles to my weary bones and mind.

Standing rigid, the waiter, with his eyes glued to the menu, followed my finger as it moved to the point I assumed was the beverage section. He listened as I slowly and carefully repeated, "Mar-teen-ee."

His eyes reflected confusion as he slowly and with great care questioned, "Maw tee nee?" We both waited silently for some breakthrough to our dilemma. He reacted first by stopping a waitress who was delivering food to an adjoining table. He lifted a plate from the tray she was carrying, pointed to its contents, and then to me, and paused and waited for my reaction. I moved my head in a negative answer. He responded by placing both arms across his chest and then raising one hand to his chin. His shoulders dropped, his head turned sideways and then faced me again.

I lifted my empty water glass, pausing briefly at face level, repeated, "mar-teen-ee" and then simulated drinking. Now he understood, and with extreme delight he uttered, while bowing graciously, "Tank uu" and departed toward the kitchen.

He glided back to my table, placed the tray on a stand, and using a linen cloth, held a container of bottled water before me for my inspection and approval. He was so sincere and expressed such a keen desire to please that momentarily I considered leaving him a generous tip and abandoning my intention.

Reconsidering that thought, I placed my glass in front of me, held up three fingers and then, in a movement that I hoped he would understand placed three imaginary ice cubes in the glass. With an imaginary bottle I filled the glass. Using a spoon handle I stirred the contents, lifted the glass to my lips, drank slowly, and then, smiling, expressed pure delight with its taste. Impressed with my own performance, I moved my eyes toward his for understanding. He bowed, pleasantly acknowledging that we had made contact, and hurriedly left.

Our conversation about the contents of my mixed drink continued with both delight and frustration. He held a bottle of bourbon before me. Taking the bottle in my hand, I nodded and said, "Yes," pointed to the label and shaking my head said, "No." With his hand firmly grasping the neck as the bottle hung at his side, he left. Next came a large bottle of Dewars Scotch. Not feeling it was necessary to say yes again, I confirmed by shaking my head and pointing at the label that scotch was not my preferred drink. The next offering was vodka and momentarily I considered changing my choice from gin to vodka. My earlier physical exhaustion had completely disappeared. My frustrating experience of trying to order gin and vermouth was replaced by a spirit of adventure. I declined the vodka.

When the gin arrived, our combined smiles confirmed progress. I held the bottle and motioned for him to go return for another bottle. He looked puzzled but somehow our newfound progress encouraged him to bring more containers to our table. After four more trips, the two prized possessions, gin and vermouth, sat in front of me. It was time for celebration. He smiled and smiled and smiled and bowed and bowed and bowed and I responded by extending the international thumbs up sign, not once, but three times.

Convinced that martinis are not part of liquid refreshment in a Chinese restaurant in Chile, I knew it would be necessary for me to mix my own. I would teach a Chinese waiter to make a Pennsylvania martini in a restaurant in Santiago, Chile. I picked up the two bottles from the table and placed them in his hands and pointed toward the kitchen. With puzzlement, he turned and walked toward that entrance.

I wanted to go to the liquor area to help him mix my drink and tried to say that. I pointed my finger, first at myself and then at him. He bowed yes, and repeated the same gesture to me. He understood, and the words he expressed certainly must have been, "You and me." I pointed across the room and he answered with a broad smile. Miracles were taking place; our understanding and communication were first class.

Smiling, bowing, and expressing some pleasant words of approval he moved behind me. I stood, he removed my chair, and I turned to face him. With a proud and confident motion his arms commanded, "Follow me." Customers at neighboring tables, who had obviously been observing our spectacle, smiled as I followed him to an archway that obviously would lead to area near the kitchen where mixed drinks were made.

With pride he turned to confirm my presence as we walked across the dining area. Shortly after entering the hallway he paused before two impressive adjoining doors. The door to our left opened and the fragrance of perfume preceded the attractive lady who walked past us. As my host leaned forward, his arm extended in front of me to open the second door, my eyes met the script on the door. I tried to read and pronounce it, "cab—all—ero." Although a journey to the men's room was not in my plans, it was timely and provided me with time to determine how to provide my tired soul with a smooth gin martini.

Returning to the dining area, I motioned for him to follow me. We walked slowly, he with hesitation and me with determination, through the door where he had returned my gin and vermouth. All the ingredients were on a shelf above a counter. First three, no maybe four, ice cubes dropped into the glass. I turned to him and smiled. The reluctant shrug of his shoulders confirmed my actions.

A slender brief flow of liquid moved from the bottle of vermouth to coat the cubes of ice. Gibson Gin, from the generous container, sparkled as it flowed over the ice into the glass. As the spoon moved in circular fashion I looked up and located a slender lemon skin. In a most articulate and professional manner, performing for my audience of one, I moved the fruit skin around the rim of the glass.

He had become a good student watching every move with intense enjoyment. Lifting my prize toward him I toasted him with, "Martini."

The perfection of his response, "Mar-teen-ee" was exceeded only by his smile.

Just Plain Dad

April 1993

9

Since my daughter's last name is not Morris, Chairman Bill Howell was surprised to see me and I could tell he was mentally searching for why I was there. When the proceedings began, my nervousness was evident as he introduced me. The applause was genuine and respectful. Feeling absolutely honored, I stood to acknowledge the recognition and momentarily questioned my decision to maintain no contact with the firm from which I had retired eight years previously.

Bill delivered an upbeat keynote address on company progress and even included, on an ad lib basis, my contributions to some of that growth. It was a proud evening, particularly for the twelve recipients of "The Chairman's Award of Excellence." A few years earlier I had been part of the team that developed this award program, but I had never received the award. Tonight, a very special person in my life would be a recipient.

After the chairman's remarks and prior to dinner being served, the honored guests, all from different states, introduced themselves. The crowd was hushed as the spotlight focused on each table, and the honored guests were handed a microphone to state their names, stores and locations, and to introduce their spouses or guests. The silence transformed to laughter as the recipients lightened their comments with political or corporate witticisms.

The overhead light moved to focus on our table, and a very proud father listened as a daughter that he had worshipped for forty years said, "My name is Susan O'Brien. I'm from Conway, Arkansas. My guest is my father and his name is "Just Plain Dad."

Only understanding the story of both the father and the daughter working in the same profession, for the same corporation, would allow you to sense my pride at that moment. The story had started twenty years earlier when my office phone rang.

"Are you too busy to talk, Popo?"

"Susan Emily! How's my favorite daughter?"

"Fine. Dad, since you folks moved to New York, I'm rattling around on weekends. Maybe I should have gone with you. But I sure do miss you all. I went to the mall where your new store is and picked up an employment application. I need something to do and thought I might get a job working Saturday and Sunday. They have an opening in fine jewelry."

"Sounds good to me."

"Dad, should I tell them that I am your daughter? There is a place on the application where you list any relatives who work for the company."

"Sure. You know I'm not ashamed of my favorite daughter. In fact, I'll call Bill LaClair and tell him you'll be in. He and I worked in Bremerton together, and that way I can check up to see if you do a good job. You know, dads have to keep track of their pretty daughters."

Our conversations after she started her part-time work were different. Maybe she thought I was more interested in what she sold, how fascinating it was to deal with the many wishes and desires of the public, how much bonus she was earning. Through frequent phone talks we developed a new, corporate, bonding.

Then one day came the announcement. "I've been

talking to Mr. LaClair about becoming a management trainee, and I think I'd like it, but... do you think I should start back East instead of Los Angeles?"

It pleased me that she was attracted to my profession, instead of nursing, and to the company that I so admired. At the same time, I was painfully aware that there was great potential for disappointment, stress, and frustration for any child who elected to follow a successful parent. In a half-hearted way I tried to discourage her but was pleased when she moved to Philadelphia and started to work as a management trainee in my company.

Sharing her progress with me on weekend visits home, she said, "Dad, I wish I could just be one of the trainees. Everybody knows that you are my dad. They treat me differently. Sometime I think they are afraid of me. Mr. Sloop, my manager, is always asking me questions about the company. He must think that you tell me all you know."

I tried to convince her that all adversities require stronger efforts and the return for that investment is greater success. She knew and I knew that in our corporate culture she would have to carry the burden of being my daughter. With interest she listened to a father's advice, "Sue, be known for what you do, not who you are."

And she did. She learned to laugh about being my daughter. Her response to inquiring questions was, "He never tells me anything." Things settled down for her, and she became "Sue" to most of her associates.

After her initial training ended she was promoted and transferred to another location in North Carolina. Again she became the daughter of a corporate officer. For lesser-performing management, her career was proof that it wasn't what you knew but who you knew that determined advancement. But Sue was good at what she was doing. She had chosen the right career; she enjoyed her work and her accomplishments spoke for themselves. For two consecutive years her results were the best of all management associates in her location and she was learning that those getting results get recognition regardless of who their fathers are.

She was in a small rural community that provided little opportunity for retail growth. She wanted to work in a large metropolitan market, and we discussed it. It just wasn't the right thing for a lower-level management associate whose father happened to be a vice president to ask for a transfer. Too many people would misunderstand it. So my little girl Sue, with confidence, determination, and a great deal of initiative, requested a leave of absence, went to metropolitan Washington, D.C., applied for a position in a new store, and was hired. On her own, at her own expense, with all her belongings in a rented U-Haul truck, she moved from Gastonia, North Carolina, to Virginia, where her father's shadow started to disappear, overcome by her own recognition.

Now retired, I proudly watched and admired her growth. What a champion she became at multiplying her efforts through people. She was not afraid to give responsibility and generously shared the results with those she supervised. During the next eight years her management abilities continued to develop. Five times she was promoted with varying and increased responsibilities. Through the media, observations from friends and through the eyes of *my favorite daughter* I watched her company continue to grow. I was pleased.

And then, almost twenty years after the phone call from Los Angeles to my office in New York I got another, important call.

"Dad, guess what? I got an invitation from Bill Howell—you know, Chairman W. R. Howell. I am going to receive the Chairman's Award of Excellence in Dallas on April 18. The invitation is for me and my spouse or guest... Would you be my date?"

That night, in Dallas, Texas, at a ceremony I will not forget, the transition was completed. Susan was no longer Will Morris' daughter. Will Morris, the retired corporate officer, bursting with pride, had become Susan O'Brien's father.

Traveling to Berea College, south of Lexington, Kentucky, was always a pleasant experience. I was privileged to be part, on a volunteer basis, of this college's mission of free education for economically disadvantaged students. I looked forward to reporting a contribution that would pay the four-year tuition for six students who would otherwise probably never have the benefits of a college experience.

With this on my mind more than the task ahead, I checked the weather and filed a flight plan from Pittsburgh's Allegheny County Airport, to Huntington, direct to Lexington and then to Berea. Although the weather forecast predicted possible scattered snow showers over Northern Kentucky, it should have been a smooth two-hour flight.

Night flying is a peaceful experience, time to be alone, suspended above God's great earth, moving toward a place and an experience. Solitude is occasionally disrupted by air traffic control reporting other aircraft in the vicinity. After passing the Huntington VOR (navigation check point) with air traffic control permission, I climbed another twelve hundred feet to assure that there would be sufficient clearance over the foothills. The moon was visible ahead of me, even though I was currently passing through a snow shower. It would have been a beautiful picture to paint.

The face of the navigation instrument panel started to

flicker. I had noticed this happening for just a few seconds passing this area on previous flights. I often wondered if there was some magnetic condition on the ground or beneath the surface. It was never a serious concern— except tonight the flight panel did not relight itself. In fact, the entire console was dark, and the interior light refused to respond. I was flying over a mountainous area, it was snowing, and if my electric power was gone, I was without radio or radar contact.

It was not time to panic but time to take inventory. My little flashlight, which I always carry when flying at night, revealed that I had plenty of gas. The engine was running smoothly, so there was no problem with power. Lexington was one hundred miles due west and I knew that I had a twenty-five mile-per-hour wind off the right nose. Air traffic control had lost radio contact, but hopefully they knew there was a metal object moving across the sky, which was a 3071Delta.

I was secure in knowing that they would keep other aircraft away from me. I banked north for ten minutes to move away from the foothills. The weather cleared, and with the aid of the non-electric compass, I headed directly west, making adjustment for the perceived 25-degree head wind. I would fly, hoping to find the lights of Lexington. If I got to Interstate 75, identifiable by all its lighted traffic, before I found Lexington, I would follow it north until I got to the Lexington airport. If I were already north of Lexington, Interstate 75 would take me to Cincinnati.

Surprisingly, I was calm. I checked my palms to confirm that they were not sweaty. Out loud I said, "Will, take it one step at a time. Find Lexington and then worry about the next step."

Lights of a city appeared ahead, and I assumed it was my destination. As I approached, I could not locate an airport beacon, nor could I identify the busy interstate.

False alarm! It was a smaller city. I didn't want to find the interstate before I found Lexington. Going north to Cincinnati would be far more risky because of commercial traffic. Time passed slowly. I wanted to see the glow of that city so badly that several times I imagined it was there. Finally, in its entire splendor, it appeared ahead of me. The closer I got the more awesome it was: ten miles of lights spreading from north to south, in contrast to my time of total darkness.

Again, I had to shout aloud, "Will, you found it!" That celebration was short-lived. Finding the airport beacon was next. Finally the flashing change of colored lights appeared to my right, so my next job was setting this little bird on the ground. I knew there were two main runways and a shorter crossing runway. My safest approach would be the shorter runway. There would be less chance that a landing jet would run up this darkened object's tailpipe. I wondered if they really knew I was here. Momentarily, my confidence disappeared.

I banked and turned to a heading of two three zero to approach runway 23. Before the turn I could see the runway lights, but until I was on final I could not see the most beautiful sight I have ever seen in my life. On each side of the runway were fire trucks with their blazing emergency lights flashing an unforgettable message to this weary, exhausted novice pilot. They were saying, "Will, come on in. Welcome to Lexington!"

What silly thoughts entered my mind in a few short seconds. I wondered what astronauts' feelings were when they returned from space. Would the local TV stations be here to record this hero's arrival? Had I violated any FAA regulations and would I be interrogated?

My wheels kissed the runway; one fire truck followed me until I stopped. Not knowing where to taxi or what to do, I turned off the engine and got out of the plane. It was

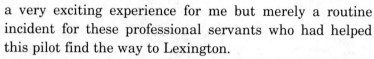

a very exciting experience for me but merely a routine incident for these professional servants who had helped this pilot find the way to Lexington.

Without electrical energy, the plane wouldn't start. Runway 23 was closed for twenty minutes while a towing vehicle arrived to take it to a hangar, where a new alternator would be installed in time for me to make my morning meeting with Rod Bussey, director of giving at Berea College.

People Don't Smile

July 1989

11

There were four of us around the simple metal table in the large sterile-looking dining hall aboard the Polish ocean ferry sailing from Gdansk, Poland, to Helsinki, Finland. William was a third-year veterinary medicine student. Zeon, a college student, was studying the economics of inland transportation. Leo, a civil engineer and very proud of his Polish heritage, taught at a university in Finland by special government permission.

Another one of the many historic intervals in Poland's unstable history was taking place. Just days before, Poland had broken free of the grasp of the Russian-controlled communist government. That government, in its fifty-year reign, had failed. It had prohibited personal initiative by a strategy that was to provide equality for all people. It had failed completely. President Bush had been in Gdansk the previous week and made a public appearance with Lech Walesa, who had been the symbol and instrument of the overthrow of the government.

Here I sat, at a table on a Polish ship with three well-educated young men, who had only known life under Polish, Moscow-controlled communism. From their parents they knew what it had been like before the German Blitz in 1939. From their limited travels and studies they had some idea of freedom—but they had never really known political freedom.

Our conversation was like a ping-pong game: back and

forth, back and forth, my inquiries about their country and their lives, and their answers, then their questions about America and my answers. They had sharp and inquisitive minds. They asked deep, penetrating, and challenging questions. The subjects ranged from economics, religious freedom, medicine, and education, to U.S. foreign aid.

They were deeply concerned with why such a great country as America would insist on paying absolute minimum prices for Poland's products and then send foreign aid in dollars to the communist-controlled government. "Wouldn't it be better to pay an acceptable value for our products, and let your financial support enter our economy at that level?" they asked. I had no answer, but I agreed with them.

Time passed rapidly as friendship and trust developed. What a privilege it was for me to be there, participating in this unstructured, candid, spontaneous conversation. Poland was probably the top story in international news and there I was just talking, and thinking aloud with people who were part of that history.

There was a pause in our conversation, and then Leo, the university teacher asked, "If you could only give me one impression of our country, what would it be?" It was Leo's question but all were interested in the answer—including me. My answer as recorded in my journal that night was: *It took several moments of thought for my reply, and I did as follows. 'I have traveled in seventeen countries this year and found no communications barrier in the use of laughter, crying and smiling. Wherever I am, regardless of language or cultural differences, when I smile it is returned and there is communication and bonding. In your country there are no smiles.'*

There was a pause as all eyes turned to Leo. Would he agree, disagree or even understand what I was trying to convey? With a sober expression on his face, he quietly and simply replied, "Yes."

The four of us were silently united in the understanding of the plight of a nation of wonderful sensitive, caring, religious, and yet *hopeless* people. This was an enormous transition of understanding for me. Prior to this unplanned five-day visit, my understanding of this country's people had been based on uncomplimentary "Polish Jokes."

In conversations with friends concerning my travels, the most often-asked question is, "Which of the fifty countries did you enjoy most?" There is no answer. Each country provided a different experience, but one thing is very certain. Poland so intrigued me that it is the only country to which I went back for a second look. I would never have wanted to miss the experience of knowing, even in my limited scope, the life of the Polish people and why there are no smiles.

As I reflect I will remember....

A once-proud nation with worthless currency, because of political changes brought on by war. I exchanged one U.S. dollar for eight hundred zlotys at the hotel desk and in the men's room of the same hotel was practically begged to exchange six thousand zlotys for a dollar. I left Poland with $122 in their currency. Aboard ship it would not buy a cup of coffee and when I landed in Helsinki it was worthless at the exchange bank.

Except for the basic needs that are produced or grown in Poland, all purchases like film, Snickers candy bars, Levi's, and Coke, must be paid for in Western currency. Poland does not have a poor economy. By our measurable standards it has no economy.[2]

As I reflect I will remember...

The pride the people have in their heritage. Not what their present condition is but what it was at one time and could be. They have dignity and stature. They are not hungry. They have food. They have brown bread, cheese, milk and poultry; and brown bread, cheese, milk and poultry; and brown bread, cheese, milk and poultry; and brown bread, cheese, milk and poultry... Fruit, except in the capital city of Warsaw, is non-existent. It is exported for the foreign currency they so desperately need.

They have clothing. They are not cold. The clothing is brown and... the clothing is brown... and *the clothing is brown*. There is no color in their scarves, shoes, or apparel. They have pride and dignity, they are not cold or hungry, but spirit and hope are missing.

As I reflect I will remember...

William. He was in line behind me as I boarded the ferry in Gdansk. He spoke English and we conversed a lot in the next thirty-seven hours. He was twenty-two years old and a veterinary medicine student in his third year of a five-year program. It was his first time away from home and he was already missing Mom and Dad back in his hometown in the south. He was on his way to Finland to work on a farm on a three-month exchange program. He would work forty hours a week and earn $6 per hour or $240. The average wage in Poland, in American dollars, was only $35 a month. From his earnings he would pay room and board, taxes to Finland and taxes to Poland, but with a dry smile on his ruddy red face, referring to his three months in Finland, he said, "I will become rich."

Under current conditions, in his profession, he will never earn enough to own an automobile.

As I reflect I will remember...

Lines of people; long lines of people. Waiting, just waiting. Waiting in front of the meat market. Waiting in line at the post office, waiting in line for the bank, the bread store, and the trolley stop. They just wait, and waiting doesn't seem to disturb them. You sense they have nothing else to do. They don't carry on conversations; they just stand. When the line moves forward they move with it and just wait. There are no smiles on their faces or in their personalities. They have little to smile about and little hope.

As I reflect I will remember...

Hope. They do have two hopes. First is their faith in God; they are a religious people. Not just religious but Christian, and they practice their belief through the Catholic Church. Poland is the only communist country that permitted the Christian faith to be openly practiced through an organized church.

Their other hope is Lech Walesa. In all my conversations I tried to get an impression of how the "man on the street" feels about Lech. His lack of formal education is countered by a very good mind. He bucked the communist party with his cause and lived to tell about it. This in itself is historic. His success, I was told, is due to his refusal to desert his cause, his own personal standards of life, his lack of desire for personal recognition, and his alignment with both the citizens and the Catholic Church. He is tough, but gentle, and has never been known to lose his temper—at least publicly.

An admirer answered my question, "Can he become president and lead your country to recovery?"

"I don't want him to. No man in his lifetime can accomplish that and I don't want him to be remembered for failure. He is too great a man."

People don't smile.

As I reflect I will remember...

No. This one I'll never forget. I've recorded my impressions of Poland not necessarily to publish them but to share them and make sure I don't forget—but I'll never forget the lady and a bright yellow banana. It was Saturday morning, and I took a train south of Gdansk, and got off at a small seaport town and walked down the main street. Nothing unusual, just early morning people walking to wherever they were going. It was wet and chilly and everyone was warmly dressed. I paused and watched a delivery truck leaving meat at a meat shop. At least thirty people were silently and patiently waiting in line. I tried to picture myself being one of them but it was beyond my comprehension.

I walked on and was startled. A little sidewalk shop and, yes, they had bananas for sale. I could not understand why the place wasn't mobbed until I remembered that a banana cost almost one day's pay.

The lady in front of me bought some bananas, paid for them in U.S. dollars and turned to walk away. She turned, stopped and looked directly into the face of another lady. This second lady, with a serious expression on her face, was tall, slender, and well-dressed in her brown apparel. She was not a beggar, nor was she destitute. She was a typical dignified Polish lady. I would have been proud to introduce her as my mother. Evidently the lady who had made the purchase sensed the importance of a banana to her. I watched as she took one and instinctively handed it to what I assumed was a total stranger and without hesitation walked on. I watched from close by. The lady cupped the banana in both her hands about waist high and looked down at it. Tears appeared and dropped from her eyes. She was overwhelmed with her good fortune.

As I reflect I will remember... Poland.

---

[2] A New York Times editorial on October 26, 1991, entitled "Why Poland Can't Flinch," quoted Lech Walesa: "We have listened to the West and made too big a leap... We have to produce even expensive things and even worse things because we have to produce, we just have to produce." The editorial went on to say: "President Lech Walesa's desperate words leading up to parliamentary elections, reflect the harsh pressure Polish politicians are under to slow the country's rush to a free market. The economy is reeling—largely because of the collapse of Soviet trade, but also because of the "shock therapy" adopted in 1990 to undo nearly five decades of centralized control.

Wanda

August, 2000

12

The exit sign, "Hancock Three Miles," caused me to remember my army buddy, John. If I left the freeway I could call to see if he was home—or even alive. I needed a pit stop and the Hancock turnoff greeted me. The C&O Canal Visitors Center on my right would surely have a restroom.

My interest in the canal was renewed as I recalled sitting at a bar in the Georgetown section of Washington where the canal ended, enjoying a scotch with a business associate and friend of thirty years. He had spoken with enthusiasm about the C&O Canal and how Supreme Court Justice William Douglas had championed its preservation. Forgetting about calling John, I read from the brochure I picked up in the visitor's center before continuing my drive: "The C&O Canal began as a dream of passage to western wealth. It operated as a conduit of eastern coal. Suffered extensive and finally fatal flooding and then resisted being paved as a highway. Today it endures as a national historical park – a pathway into history, nature and recreation."

Back to the freeway, with the countryside passing, I could only think of the canal. One hundred eighty-five miles from Cumberland, Maryland to Georgetown, Washington, D.C. Seventy-five lift locks elevating it six hundred nine feet, and a twelve-foot wide towpath along its south bank. Could I hike it? Ridiculous—my knees ache going up the stairs to bed.

A few days later, with my newly-purchased backpack filled with thirty-five carefully weighed pounds of cargo, I tried a seven-mile trial hike. The aching ankles, blisters on my toe, and tenderness on my shoulders dictated that the weight would need to be reduced at least ten pounds. My next ten-mile test produced more blisters, but less ankle and knee discomfort.

For fear of ridicule, I could only share this outlandish scheme with my wife. We selected supplies that would only weigh twenty-five pounds, which would more likely ensure success—even though we both knew I would never undertake hiking 185 miles: sleeping bag, container for water, twelve power bars, three throw-away cameras, plastic tarp, plastic cover and a worn-out beach towel for nighttime warmth; also "The C&O Canal Companion," a complete guide to the history of the C&O. My first aid supply kit contained aspirin, knee supports, ankle supports, insect repellent, a multitude of band-aids, and— as insurance, even if it exceeded the weight limit—six little airline bottles of Johnny Walker.

Bikers, completing a three-day ride from the start of the canal, exited the trail at Cumberland where the canal, the Potomac River and railroad terminal linked. With complete confidence that this foolish venture would end before sunset, I entered the towpath and made the first of the 357,930 steps that would take me to the mouth of Rock Creek in Georgetown.

The first of the one hundred eighty-five mile markers that I hoped to pass appeared. It was a matter of success or failure. I was on my way. At marker 182 the distraction of the city gave way to the silence of the countryside. The highway, the river and the sounds and sights of people disappeared. The towpath and the canal, filled with the aroma of stagnant green water, formed the base of a tunnel that was completed by the overhanging branches of the trees.

I was alone, and mentally in the world of the past—the time when the canal was being created. George Washington, as a sixteen-year-old apprentice surveyor, had a vision of a canal along the Potomac, across the mountains and connecting with the Ohio River. I was no longer a hiker from the twentieth century, but part of an engineering miracle. Just walking along this path made me a part of the history of the Chesapeake and Ohio Canal that had started before we became a nation.

Will, lost in part of history

It was a hot day and as I walked past mile markers 181, then 180 and 179, my shirt became wet with perspiration and my ankles tender. The next marker did not appear as quickly as the last one. Passing a marker did not shorten my journey. It reminded me that the balance of this journey was a long way, a very long way, to Georgetown. Seven miles from my start I came to a small campground and water pump at Evitts Creek. I filled my quart plastic bottle with fresh water and then drank it all to satisfy my thirst and lessen the weight. Stripping to the waist, I pumped water over my head, face and upper torso.

My increasing fatigue faded as I observed the seventy-foot aqueduct that allowed the Evitts Creek waters to flow beneath the canal and towpath. I sat on a ledge above the water and focused my eyes on where the creek emerged from the green forest. My mind was focused on history, the activity of building this structure one hundred sixty years ago. In my imagination I watched the workers build the one and a half-mile wooden railroad up Evitts Creek, where the compact limestone filled with marine shells was quarried. The screech of the horse-drawn scoops digging the canal and forming its banks, scraping against solid rock, sent chills down my spine. The sounds of the workers, shouting, commanding and encouraging, drifted into the silent forest. Beneath me and beneath the old canal bed, the waters of Evitts Creek flowed on their journey to the Potomac, just as they had in 1837. My journey this day was to reach mile marker 156 and the Heritage Trail Bed & Breakfast. So I returned to the present, to fatigue, tender ankles and shoulders, and twenty-two more miles of towpath before sunset. I was only one fourth of the way and it was two hours past high noon.

Farther down the towpath I stopped to rest. A three-person bicycle trail patrol approached and stopped. Their questions, "Are you all right? Are you alone? Do you have food and water?" did little to relieve my fatigue or brighten my confidence.

"Yes, and I'm fine," was an overstatement. The patrol assured me that it would be safe to camp at the campsite at lock # 75, the first lock I would pass. It was still three-mile markers to the lock, and many more steps to the Heritage Trail Bed & Breakfast.

Lock # 75 completed the task of what the other 74 had started and supported, lifting the canal the last ten of the six hundred and nine foot elevations necessary to have a waterway to the west. As majestic as this mortared gray limestone was, my thoughts did not center on its construction but on its function those many years ago. I sat by the lock and visualized what would have taken place during its productive time: The lock keeper had lived with his family in the lock house, provided by the C&O Company. The sound of a horn broke the silence, along with a loud reply from the lock keeper saying, "Lock ready! Lock ready!" A pair of mules appeared, followed by a canal boat separated by a 100-foot towline. The mules stopped, without instructions or control, as the bow of the boat came to the entrance of the lock. The lock keeper, his wife, the boat captain and two members of his crew helped guide the boat as the team of mules responded to verbal encouragement and gently pulled it into the lock. The large gates closed and water from upstream entered the lock.

The atmosphere changed. The boat captain bought hay for his mules, fresh vegetables, milk, and firewood for the cook stove from the lock keeper who supplemented his $200 annual income by growing these items on the acre of land that the C&O granted. This transaction took place during the ten minutes required to change the water level.

The lower gates opened and with a command "come up" from the driver the mules' rest ended, and they reluctantly tightened the towline and moved their cargo toward the next lock. As the boat cleared the lock, I climbed aboard. The canal boat was ninety-five feet long — five feet shorter than the lock. Its fourteen and one half-foot width left only a three-inch clearance on each side as it passed through the lock. Its cargo was coal, loaded at the rail yards in Cumberland for the four-day, eighteen-hour-a-day trip to Georgetown.

The captain, who lived in family quarters with his wife and four children, had been on a canal boat since he was seven. He inherited the canal boat from his father. His two teenage sons worked as mule driver and boat tender. His wife was the cook. There were two tricks of mules. One trick ate and rested in the mule shed on the front of the boat while the second one provided the power for the trip. Hay and feed were kept in the mule shed. The teenage sons used the hay for their beds.

I needed to rest some more, but if I was going to get to the B&B the blisters had better start feeling the gravel towpath. It was eleven miles to Old Town. My book described the amenities as a small country store on Main Street that offered ice cream, sandwiches and canned goods. The thought of a sandwich reminded me that I was hungry, so I consumed another bar and started walking. I tried to determine whether my lack of energy or muscle soreness was more distressing. They were equal.

As I continued, my exhaustion and aching overcame my enthusiasm. I was three miles past the last campsite and three miles from the next one. The only choice was to try to make the next one. As I rounded a bend in the towpath my eyes ached as I searched for the next mile marker. Somehow I reached the campsite. It consisted of a water pump, a wooden picnic table and a small open spot of grass. Not a comfortable place to stay. I needed to be closer to some form of civilization, so after a fresh drink and another power bar, which didn't even taste good, I pressed on.

After wishing I had never made that pit stop in Hancock two weeks earlier, I played a mind game even though my body objected. There were five miles to go; after the first grueling mile there was one mile behind me and four in front. Somehow I struggled to the next mile marker. Reason to celebrate... almost halfway there? Then the third mile and now it would be downhill. But it wasn't. It taxed every ounce of my depleting energy to pick up a foot and place it ahead of the other one. At the fourth mile I sat down and took the moleskin padding out of my shoes. The soles of my feet were painfully tender, and adding to the discomfort, my feet were swelling.

While walking the last mile, my spirits somehow overcame the hurt. It takes 1840 steps for me to walk a mile, so I walked one hundred step segments eighteen times. The last steps brought me to a white lock house where a small bridge crossed the canal. Two small boys, their bicycles on the bridge, were fishing in the canal. A sign near the bridge said "Old Town."

"Is there a general store near here?" I asked.

"About half a mile out to the road and then to your right," they replied.

Somehow the tight muscles relaxed more quickly as I walked to the general store and set my pack beneath a pay phone on the front porch. Mom and Pop, the obvious owners, were the only people in the store. I wanted a beer but settled for a Dr. Pepper, the only beverage available. A middle-aged man, a customer, entered the store and asked if they had a six-inch cotter pen.

"No we don't, but you might find something in that box of stuff." He walked to the rear of the store where the box was located.

The soft drink was cooling and I was at the general store, but frankly I didn't know what my next step was. Mom and Pop assured me there was no lodging in town. My pulse was pounding and my body trembling. I didn't know what to do. Trying to sleep on the porch was an option. What if they found my body there the next morning?

The customer, unable to find his item, walked to the door and left. I followed him to the porch, and for some reason, pleading as boldly as my strength allowed, I blurted, "Sir." When he turned around I finished my desperate request, "I am seventy-five years old and I have

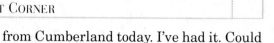

walked the canal from Cumberland today. I've had it. Could you take me to Paw Paw?"

There was a questioning pause, then a partial smile and, "I might. My dog is in my car; I'll need to take him home first. I'll be back in a couple minutes."

Waiting for his return, I phoned the Heritage Trail B&B in Paw Paw and confirmed lodging. My half-hour ride included an enthusiastic narration of the C&O. My driver was proud of the history of the canal. We crossed the Potomac to the West Virginia side and he delivered me to the B&B. He carried my backpack to the door, rang the bell and set the pack inside. I folded two twenty and ten-dollar bills in my hand, knowing no amount of money could express my appreciation.

"Oh, I can't take anything for this. Glad to help you." I waited at his car window to assure him how much I appreciated what he had done. A bible was laying on the seat beside him. He was my Good Samaritan, not on the road from Jerusalem to Jerico but on the road from Old Town to Paw Paw.

The owner, addressing me as Mr. Morris, said my room was up the stairs and to the right. While she was explaining about the bath, the towel and morning breakfast, I was wondering if I could carry the pack up the stairs. I couldn't, and with my hostess watching in amazement, I shamefully crawled up the stairs, and entered the air-conditioned bedroom, and somehow managed to get on the bed. The first day of my hike on the C&O ended.

Wanda served breakfast, not the power bars and plastic water bottles of yesterday, but china, linen napkins, ice water in crystal, orange juice, cantaloupe, bacon, Belgian waffles, and steaming coffee from a silver pot. My hostess was both gracious and interesting. She was eighty years old and forty years a widow. The B&B was her livelihood.

"I was called to be a nurse," she said as she showed me her expanded home that included three rooms for personal care patients. She had three residents—"girls," she called them. Her favorite girl was eighty-four years old. Her husband had died and left her with five young children. Twenty-three years ago, when she could no longer care for herself, the children had placed her in Wanda's care. It had been fifteen years since any of her children had visited her. Returning to the breakfast table, listening to the remainder of her story, I knew I had met an angel. She was fulfilling her calling with great joy.

I said goodbye to Wanda, kissed her on the cheek and continued my journey. The 3,118 foot Paw Paw tunnel, the result of eleven years digging through solid rock, was half a mile away. The tunnel was dark. The wooden rail that years ago had supported the towline and kept the mules on the path, guided me from the dark interior to the opening and the bright sunlight. It was the second day of my adventure and there were one hundred fifty-five more mile markers to pass.

Tenth Birthday
February 2002

13

The joyous party on February 7, 2002 had its sober moments. Our forty-seven-year-old John was celebrating his tenth birthday with his parents, his wife Theresa, and his seventeen-year-old son Ryan. Each year that passed was another important step to the tenth, and it had finally arrived. There was a lot to celebrate. The party included dinner, with fine wine, at the Mozart Room, a night at the symphony, and thankful remembrances of the past ten years. Interwoven throughout the celebration were personal reflections of the people who had been instrumental in helping a man with strands of gray in his hair celebrate his tenth birthday. Their stories and involvement, spread over a twenty-five year period, made them all a part of this tenth birthday celebration.

It had started years ago when John's concerned parents sat with their family physician, Dr. Frank Rosendale, and he asked, "Tell me as best you can recall what happened last night."

"We heard John gasping like he was choking. He was thrashing all over his bed, shaking violently. Every muscle in his body seemed to be exploding. We could not hold him in place. When the upheaval stopped he just lay limp with heavy breathing."

In a calm, peaceful way the family doctor explained. "From your description John had an epileptic seizure. The impulses in his brain are taxed beyond their capacity, and like an electric current they short out. This malfunction in the brain causes a seizure and affects some part of the body. In the severe, grand mal form the original short is intensified and expanded to include larger portions of the brain, resulting in convulsions and unconsciousness, and followed by intense lingering headache."

"Frank, what causes them to short out?"

"Medically, we don't know. It's a disease or condition of the nervous system. If we knew, we might find a cure. From what we know today, there is no known cure. We just try to control or eliminate the seizures by medication. Unfortunately, medication that controls the seizures often severely dulls responses."

Ruth and I departed in silence. Footsteps were muted, and the click of the closing office door was the only sound, including the ride home.

Medication reduced the number of seizures; different medication reduced them further. The addition of a third medication caused them to cease until body growth caused the drugs to be partially ineffective. More medicine overcame the effects of body growth but produced far more lack of energy, dulled senses and reactions. For the next twenty-five years, John's life was a conflict between a disease that prevented a normal life, and the medication that controlled the disease—assuring that his life would not be a normal one. Yet John, with his spirit and ability to accept and live with his handicap, led a normal life.

His school grades were acceptable. Playing the French horn in his high school orchestra fulfilled his interest in music. Because he was controlled by medication, he was able to drive a car until a tragic accident, caused by an epileptic seizure, almost cost him his life. The handicap of needing to be chauffeured to work and wherever he went would be a lifelong reminder of not being whole. In his fourth year of college he performed, to his parents' standing ovation, in a college drama. Marriage followed college, as did two children and a career in retailing.

The contest between a life of heavy medication and the dulling effect it had on his mental capacity continued to be an issue for John and his family. At a clinic in North Carolina, where the build up of toxic drugs—accumulated over long periods—were being eradicated from his body, he first learned about research in surgery that was sometimes successful in eliminating epileptic seizures.

John's Dayton, Ohio, neurologist, Dr. Allen Jacobs, was familiar enough with the research project to describe the parameters to the family. "We know what we have today. Your activities are limited; we cannot see any cure at the present time, but you have been very successful in providing an acceptable lifestyle for your family. It's a given; we know what we have."

Their silence acknowledged understanding and agreement as Dr. Jacobs continued, "First, it's very expensive, and because it is recognized as experimental, insurance normally doesn't cover the cost. You could be away from work up to six months. If testing results eliminate you as a candidate, the process could be terminated at any point, and you would be back to where you are today."

"Doctor, what percent of the people who enter the program are successful?"

"I don't know. I do know that each day a panel of twelve doctors that specialize in epilepsy reviews the testing results. Neurologist Dr. Sutherland and brain surgeon Dr. Michael Levesque chair this panel. If any one of this twelve-member panel voices concern that the surgery would not prove successful, the project goes no further."

Again the room was filled with silence until, "What are they looking for in these tests?"

"John, in your case the seizure takes place in some area

of your brain. What makes your version so severe is that it explodes to a larger portion, or—we really don't know—maybe the entire brain. That is why your seizures are so severe and affect so many parts of your body. If they can locate where the seizure starts and determine that that section does not affect a vital function, they can remove it and thus eliminate the origin. If this happens you could be seizure-free for the balance of your life."

"Doctor, that sounds good, but what are the downsides?"

"Let me say this, from what I've read—and I've never met or talked to these two doctors—you, your family and children would be asked to sign a release of liability for this procedure, so there are serious risks. Results range from total elimination of epilepsy, to remaining on current medication, to the possibility of failure and becoming totally handicapped for the remainder of your life. My understanding is that the UCLA Medical Center in Los Angeles has the most recognized program in the country."

On the drive home the last of Dr. Jacobs's words, "It is a decision that only you can make," refused to leave their thoughts.

John and his family needed support, and as his father, I joined the team. My first task was to contact Dr. David Gluck, medical director of the corporation I was associated with for over thirty years. Dave was a trusted friend. We had counseled on many corporate medical situations, and he had been most helpful in locating the facility in North Carolina where the build-up of toxic drugs was cleansed from John's system. I had asked him to research and confirm my son's doctor's recommendation.

"Will, John's doctors are right. The UCLA Medical Center has the best record of success for this type of procedure in the country and perhaps the world. If he can be helped, they are his best bet."

"If both you and John's neurologist feel that this is the best facility and he and his family want to undertake it, we'll proceed. Dave, thanks for you help. You'll never know how much the Morris family appreciates all the support you have given John."

With a balance of confidence and apprehension, but an overwhelming desire for an improved quality of life, John's family decided to put themselves in the hands of the project team at University of California Los Angeles Medical Center. The next three months were an excursion into the realm of the medical unknown for John and his family. Neurologist Dr. William Sutherland, a talented medical scientist and key member of the research team, explained the procedure that, if successful, would reduce the severity of or totally eliminate his seizures. This would require identifying any part of the brain where seizures originated that did not affect vital functions, memory, body movement, sight, touch, and even personality, and surgically removing that portion. To accomplish this, his skull would be opened and 178 platinum electrodes would be placed on his brain to record the impulses. These electrodes would be connected to a computer that would confirm where a seizure started and how it expanded into the other segments of the brain. How he reacted when a seizure occurred would be recorded on a monitor. This would take up to thirty days or until it was determined that he would or would not be a candidate for the surgery.

To this very professional medical staff, John along with the dozen other patients, was a subject. The staff were scientists and their goal was to find relief for the multitude of people on this earth who suffered from this condition. That was not the case with Jody Smyth. She was a feisty, witty, brilliant young nurse from the Midwest who had attended college at UCLA and migrated into this Epilepsy Research Unit. Her specialty and responsibility were to locate the center of the seizures through the measurement and locations of the impulses from the brain. She stood at the elevator with the family as the gurney entered and the journey to the operating room started. John's reassuring smile and thumbs-up signal did not prevent the family silence and moist eyes—Jody's among them. She explained again that his skull would be opened and 178 electrodes would be secured to his brain. She saw John not as a subject, but as a person, and she was already a member of his growing family. I walked back toward the sterile room where she worked, but was halted by a sign on the glass wall that read, "Be Realistic, Expect a Miracle."

For two weeks Jody tirelessly worked to connect the electrodes, through the seventeen wires extending from beneath John's skull, to the computer and onto the video cameras. When a seizure occurred, the computer recorded where it originated, and the camera recorded the body movements that resulted from it. Her partner was Paul. He was working for the first-ever Ph.D. in computer neurology. His responsibility was to verify that the computer correctly identified the affected brain area and the video recorded the movement that was generated in that area.

For the next ten days, John was forced to go without sleep, his medicine was eliminated, he went without food, was given the wrong food, was startled, was shouted at, slapped on the face, pinched—all punishment that would force him to have seizures. This went on twenty-four hours a day and was recorded both on the computer and film.

The twelve-member project team met each morning at ten, and after Paul had assured them that the data was valid, they elected by unanimous vote to proceed or abort the project. There were six candidates in various stages of testing. Each family and patient waited for his or her decision. When patients were eliminated, sadness prevailed in the little community as they and their families received the news and departed. Some walked, some were in wheelchairs, and some were so taxed with this ailment that they were not aware of what was taking place. As they and their families departed, the hope absent from their faces, new candidates with new hope eagerly took their place in the bonding family.

After thirty days, in late November, all tests were done. Dr. Sotherland's words will stay embedded in our minds forever: "John is a good candidate, and we will proceed."

On December 17, the electrodes were removed, and that section of the brain where seizures originated was resectioned. The best medical knowledge and skill in our country had determined that the area where the seizures originated, and spread to the major part of the brain, could be surgically removed and not affect John's speech, memory or body movement. We prayed that they were right.

The surgery, compared to the testing and evaluation period, was minor. John was discharged the day before Christmas and returned home for a year of waiting for results. His brain needed to heal. After one year his medication would be gradually reduced to determine the degree of success. It could be no improvement, improvement to the point of requiring less medication (thus enabling him to lead a more normal life), or total elimination of his seizures. John's final epileptic seizure, a very mild one, occurred February 7, 1992, seven weeks after surgery.

Driving was a symbol of not being an invalid. It had been degrading to be driven to and from work and any place he needed to be. After one year of seizure-free life, the state of Ohio issued John a driver's permit that allowed him to drive with another adult present. After fifteen years, he learned to drive again. During the second year he passed driver's exams and with his neurologist's assurance that he was seizure-free, he could legally operate a car. I went to Ohio for a visit, and John reported to work late that morning because we were car shopping. At a Ford agency he picked out a gold-colored Probe sports car with a stick shift and all the trimmings. I gleefully picked up the tab and followed him off the lot. He turned left, and I watched as he drove down the street to work. I turned right for the four-hour ride home but could not move from the driveway. Unashamed tears flowed down my face as I thanked God that my son was a whole person again.

John drove his automobile from Dayton to Pittsburgh for his tenth birthday party. It was a joyous occasion but saddened because some special people could not attend. Our neighbor, Della, now deceased, had received our daily phone report for all those days at the hospital and relayed it to our prayer partners. We don't know their names but a group of ladies at North Side Christian Church had met daily and prayed for the hands that connected the electrodes and performed the surgery. Science, medicine and faith were all at work. As nurse Jody knew, it was realistic to expect a miracle.

The joy of the occasion was saddened by the absence of John and Theresa's daughter Miranda. She had been a sweet nine-year-old girl during the time in UCLA. She had waited in the hospital rooms, not totally understanding what was taking place. One thing was sure; she wanted Dad to get well. On November 16, 2000, Miranda, a sophomore at Bowling Green University, died in the shower in her dormitory from an epileptic seizure. Science, research, dedicated people and faith had restored a life. A dreadful, unconquered disease had taken another life from the same family.

Hateful Defiance

November 1989

14

The country road that had passed through a small village abruptly ended in the courtyard of a large stone building. Three small children timidly approached my car. Their stares were penetrating. They refused to return my smile but readily accepted the fresh oranges that I had bought in Bethlehem that morning. They snatched the fruit from my hand and defiantly turned their backs as if to indicate that the fruit belonged to them and I had never had right of ownership. I left the courtyard and retraced my journey down the narrow mountainous road across the dry rocky countryside, and back to the village.

Small children threw rocks at my car after I passed them. Remembering throwing a rock at a passing car and getting in serious trouble with my parents, I thought, "Kids are the same the world over."

Adults staring suspiciously and standing motionless along the road caused anxiety to creep over me. Palestinian flags were displayed even though they were prohibited. Something was not right.

Leaving the village and more occupied with my concerns than my driving, I slowed my speed and touched the brakes. Boulders had been placed across the road from the dry rocky banks that rose substantially above me on either side. It was a well-defined roadblock. The road was too narrow for me to turn around. I was a prisoner. Young Palestinian youth stood atop the banks on each side of the road with large rocks in a ready position, perhaps waiting for a signal to begin their attack.

I had rented the little white Ford Escort that morning at a hotel in Jerusalem and driven to Bethlehem. I was still searching for a little of that "Godly" feeling that surely must exist in the birthplace of Christianity. Coming to Jerusalem to experience the Holy Land could have been a mistake. I had expected the tourist interests to point with pride to the birthplace of Christ, and the people I met to speak with pride of the Christian heritage of their country. Pride was nowhere to be found. The peddlers were just as aggressive as they were in the seaport cities of Istanbul and Tangier. Armed soldiers were plainly visible.

Conversations and newspaper accounts centered on the conflict and hatred between the Arabs and Jews. Both nationalities felt the land rightfully belonged to them. The Arabs deeply resented the Jews being given their homeland. They had been pushed into separate areas and had none of the privileges of having their own government. They were not allowed to bear arms or even display their flag, so their symbol and weapon of defiance was "the rock." Their voice of opposition was to hurl rocks.

Another obvious part of this conflict was the uncompromising difference in Christian, Jewish, and Muslim religious beliefs. The religious laws of Jews and Arabs were a dominant part of their life and government. Israel—or at least Jerusalem—was a festering, boiling pot from both political and religious points of view.

When I had departed Bethlehem earlier for the Dead Sea, I was excited to be "going down from Jerusalem to Jericho." The story of the Good Samaritan in the tenth chapter of Luke entered my mind. In fact I did pass a very modern, commercial "Good Samaritan Inn."

Continuing to look for adventure, I had turned off the main highway onto a small country road in a more eastern direction toward the Dead Sea. The countryside was dry and barren and the few people that I saw stood motionless, almost like statues. I wondered if a car traveling this road was such a rarity that they froze to stare at it.

As I entered a village, driving very slowly, several small children positioned themselves in front of my car and expected or demanded, by their lack of expression, that I stop. They stood just inches away. I attempted to communicate with smiles and gestures that I wanted to pass but they stood firm. In other countries their hands would have been held out for money, but there were no little hands extended here. Without facial or body expression they just stood their ground. I very slowly inched forward, expecting them to move aside. Only after persistent effort was I allowed to move on. I don't recall seeing any adults, and if there were any they did not encourage or discourage the incident.

Now I was stopped at the roadblock waiting. Waiting for what... I did not know. Even though I knew this was trouble, my calm surprised me. The first rock landed directly on the road in front, only to be followed by a thunderous crash on the top of the car. There was nothing I could do. I instinctively locked both doors and waited. Both windows on my right side took direct hits, but stones did not enter the car. The right side of the windshield was shattered and small fragments of glass fell on the seat. This continued for several minutes. Each of my attackers, from both sides of the road, had a pile of weapons he intended to use. The sounds of rocks meeting steel and glass stopped just as abruptly as it had begun. The silence was painful.

I opened the door and got out to move the rocks that blocked my way. Keeping a sharp eye for the possibility of renewed activity, I moved four stones from the path of the car, got back in and continued my journey. Driving steadily but cautiously to the safety of open country, I wondered, "Did I take full insurance coverage on the rental car? Why was I singled out for a rock attack? Did the rock throwing stop because they feared I might be armed?"

Stopping, I got out to take a better look at the car. It was a disaster. The damage did not have the depth of a serious impact but the car had been wounded. Both its personality and dignity had been destroyed. After reporting to the Jerusalem police and returning to my small hotel room, I reflected on the day's experience. The rocks, the breaking glass, the damage to the car—which had taken thirteen direct hits—became unimportant. I had to try to understand why this had happened. I had been part of a small frame of the life of a few Palestinian youth. Like others, it was a story of circumstances.

A few days earlier on a bus ride from Cairo to Jerusalem I had shared a seat with Abla and Essa Bateh. They were both born in Ramallah and had met in Jacksonville, Florida, at the age of fourteen. They were returning to Ramallah to visit relatives. At the border they listed their nationality as Palestinian instead of American. They were labeled and although they could talk to their relatives by phone the Israeli government refused to allow their entry into Ramallah. At dinner that night they helped me understand what had happened to this farm boy on November 18, 1989.

I was a victim of the Arab's "weapon of defiance," the rock. My car, rented in Jerusalem, had a yellow license plate, which indicated that it was Israeli. All alone, I had invaded Palestinian territory and while the adults tolerated my presence, the youth retaliated against me. Not me personally, but the person in the car with the yellow license plate.

There is a deeper force and meaning to explain why I was stoned. The boiling hatred and mistrust in this unusual country has been developed and nurtured over the centuries. Like all people, each new generation is exposed to the values of their parents and their parents' parents. They are reared in a climate of understanding: "My religious belief is right and yours is wrong, therefore you are bad." "I was in this land first, and you arrive and tell me it is yours." "My religion tells me we are a chosen people and this land is ours because God meant for us to have it." "Because the only recourse is to fight against what we think is wrong, we fight back." "You are bad and we learn to hate. Hatred grows and we forget why we hate. We just hate."

Arabs take the lives of other Arabs because some drift toward more liberal attitudes and are destroyed to preserve the strength of hatred toward the Jews. National leaders refuse to talk to the other side because that would show a weakness to the cause. Young adult minds are occupied with revenge for a cause that came with their birth and in all probability they don't understand. It goes on and on. And innocent little children, with an abundance of hatred in their hearts, which you can see in their eyes, throw rocks without knowing why. Hatred and vengeful defiance go on in this land of strange circumstances where Christians understand that Love was born.

Return to Helmstedt

July 1989

15

"This is going to be a great day for me! I am traveling by train, across Communist East Germany, from West Berlin to the little German town of Helmstedt. Forty-four years ago, Sergeants John Spitzer and Everett Downing, Corporal Paul Kiefer and I were the first enemy soldiers to enter this village. I remember the stone train station and the post office. Wonder if they will look the same today?"

Almost unaware that the train was leaving West Berlin Zoo station, my mind moved back to being that twenty-year-old soldier in Helmstedt. It was just another one of many little German towns that had suffered the hunger and devastation of the Second World War, however I would not forget the empty stares of the women, children and older men. Air strikes, death of families, and fear of their enemies had been reality, but now their fear was realized. Four American soldiers were in their midst. The looks on their faces reflected the fright of seeing their enemy.

The remnants of Hitler's dispirited army were ten miles east. There were still skirmishes but everyone knew that Germany was a defeated nation. We were very cautious as our two vehicles entered Helmstedt and slowly traveled its cobblestone streets.

"Sure don't want to get shot today," Corporal Kiefer, who was driving our truck loaded with communication gear, thought out loud. We both knew the war was unofficially over, and what a tragedy a loss of life would be

107

from this point forward. Our mission was to find telephone circuits back to our division headquarters located forty kilometers west. They would be located in the postal building if it had remained intact, which seemed likely since the German retreat had been rapid.

The building was up a small hill from the railroad station. The nervous chief of communication, in his military uniform, with fearful respect, understood our demands. He delivered the telephone and telegraph circuit blueprint and the keys to the cable vault. This was all we needed—the heart of the communications system. With the arrogance of captors we followed him through the facility, ending at the third floor apartment where he and his wife and son lived.

Sgt. Morris and three other American soldiers took control of this building in Helmstedt as WWII wound down

We had what we needed: the keys to the building, the blueprint of the circuits, and his apartment. We asked, or demanded, that he and his family take their personal belongings and leave. They were the enemy and we were the captors. Without any concern for their comfort or dignity we celebrated. Our sleeping bags would be replaced by mattresses, sheets, and quilted comforters. We hoped that this would be our home until the end of the war, but there was work to do. Sergeants Downing and Spitzer, in businesslike manner, attacked the cable vault. Paul and I were to scout the nearby area in our truck. Corporal Paul Kiefer was an Indiana farm boy, and like mine, his life had been decidedly altered by his local draft board. He was an unusual example of the physical requirements necessary to win a war. He was overweight, flat-footed, and the soles of his feet were a constant abscess of bunions... all good qualifications to become our truck driver. Instead of a normal look-around-town excursion, Paul seemed to have a specific destination in mind.

"Where are we going?"

"Braunschweig. A tanker told me there was a brewery there and I haven't had a beer in thirteen months."

Paul liked beer. All GIs missed something most of all: home, a juicy steak, family, wife or girlfriends. Paul missed beer. He didn't like it; he loved it. Half an hour later and across the countryside we stood before the guarded iron gates of a brewery entrance. "We want beer."

One of the two guards departed, returned with two green bottles of beer, and nervously handed them to us. We uncompromisingly "requisitioned" a keg, put it on our truck and sarcastically thanked the uniformed German guards. Our priority mission, having switched from identifying communication circuits to finding beer, had succeeded. On the triumphant ride back to town, Paul was all smiles; he had "the smile of beer" until a serious frown replaced the smile.

"We don't have a keg tap."

With the prize in the basement, three floors below our

yet-to-be-used furnished apartment, Paul and I formed a search party. Downing and Spitzer assured us they would defend the keg with their lives. The search started by just knocking on doors. Doors opened; disturbed and concerned residents waited for the worst from two enemy soldiers.

"A beer tap?"

What a strange war this was. Soldiers on both sides of this conflict were still fighting and dying, world leaders were trying to find an appropriate way to end the war and our war—here in this little German town that only short hours ago had been invaded by American soldiers—was to find a tap for our keg of beer. Down some dark street, we claimed one from a very fearful tavern owner.

Securing the circuit blueprints, the keys to the cable vault and the building were of minor importance compared to the ceremony of the tapping of the keg. Even sleeping on a mattress upstairs under a comforter came in a distant second. The four of us discussed the strategy of tapping a small wooden keg of German beer. How we would react if there were a problem was of more concern than entering this village had been this very morning. John and I tenderly held our patient while surgeon Paul inserted the tap that would free the contents.

The pump handle lowered as the brown liquid flowed into the aluminum canteen cup. Never before had this cup held such precious fluid. Paul looked at it, lifted the cup to his lips, and tasted it. Twenty-four hours later the keg was empty. Most of it had gone into Paul's body and renewed his spirits. That afternoon and during the night his trips to the basement, canteen cup in hand, were interrupted only by very short naps and necessary trips to the bathroom.

Daily, human tragedies of war walked by our building. They moved like a stream of water along the street, past the train station and up the hill in front of our new residence. They were refugees from German labor camps.

and prisons, and German citizens who had been displaced during this conflict, trying to return to their homes or to where their homes had been. Pushing bicycles loaded with all they owned, pulling loaded carts, and burdened with their belongings on their backs, they passed by from morning until night, returning to their unknown futures.

I could only look, only imagine the circumstances of their plights. When they turned their pitiful faces toward me, my hand seemed to raise automatically into a friendly wave, only hoping that they understood that I was trying to understand and that assuredly for all of us the war was ended. I was startled at a voice, "Hi Yank"—coming from a hunch-backed old man pushing a bike loaded with his belongings slowly up the hill from the train station. He had been born in Ohio and returned to Germany with his parents when he was sixteen. Although a German citizen, he had spent the war as conscripted labor in a munitions factory.

That was the Helmstedt I knew then. War had started for me with the draft board notice, received after my eighteenth birthday, and had ended in Helmstedt. I had changed, and history had changed Helmstedt. For me, it would never be "just another little German town."

No longer a soldier, but back home on the farm, contemplating college, I had explained to my proud father that the newly-revealed border dividing Germany into two nations passed through the little town where I had been when war ended. Dad listened with interest as I told him how President Truman, Winston Churchill and Stalin had honored the little town that I had "captured."

Later in college we discussed world politics that followed the war. The demilitarized zone from Berlin to West Germany started at "my" little town. In a college class at the university we were actually talking about the significance of Helmstedt. All land traffic halted here, at the Russian checkpoint, before starting its journey across Communist East Germany to the free city of West Berlin. My pride must have been apparent as I described the railroad station and the autobahn entrance for my classmates.

My life continued to change. The world continued to change. I was learning to pin diapers on my newborn son when the first confrontation crisis of the Cold War was news the world over. The world saw it on television; and cameras recorded what took place, and I saw Helmstedt on television. Russian tanks blocked both the entrance to the station and the autobahn. Within hours, the historic Berlin Airlift delivered food, fuel and clothing to imprisoned West Berlin.

The Cold War had already lasted forty years and to my mind it had started in Helmstedt. The conductor asked for my ticket. I had forgotten that I was on a train. It was a struggle to make the mental return from my thoughts of Helmstedt's transition to a town of distinction, back to being a sixty-five-year-old traveler trying to locate a train ticket.

The train slowed, passed a sign, "Helmstedt One Kilometer," and then the station appeared. Time had not altered its appearance. Struggling with the conflict of reliving my town as it had been, or seeing it as it was, I slowly walked up the hill. The steps where I had sat watching the crowds of refugees when the old man had said "Hi, Yank" were unchanged, but the building had a modern—uncomfortable for me—addition to it.

I was alone and wanted to be. I was here to see and compare. My story should be told, but to whom would I tell it? How would the people react to the return of an enemy soldier? Would they resent me? Would my presence be a symbol of deaths of families and destruction of belongings? This unknown fascinated me, and yet I just wanted to stand here and imagine what might happen.

That evening I walked around "my" town. I found the

town square, sat on the post office steps, and even found the tavern that might have supplied the keg tap. I enjoyed a beer, weinerschnitzel and a restful night's sleep.

A military office, RIO Allied Forces, at the train station was supervised by a Scottish civilian, Mr. Vincent, who was a NATO employee. Maybe he was intrigued with my shoulder length hair, baggy jeans and canvas shoes but he listened with interest. He was the Allied NATO official responsible for the entry into today's Berlin corridor, which was still controlled by Russian communist forces. My story had taken place before he was born and he enjoyed hearing about this part of the town's history.

"Would you know anybody who could take me through the old building where I lived?"

He dialed his phone, talked with enthusiasm in a language that I couldn't understand, put the phone back in its cradle and said, "Let's go."

Hans Betzholtz, the postmaster, greeted me with a warm handshake. My host, in German, shared my story, including how we had occupied the third-floor apartment. He eagerly toured us through the post office. The friendly workers smiled and shook my hand as he told them who I was and why I was there.

Walking up the stairs to the third floor, I remembered Paul climbing these same stairs, big smile on his face, licking the foam from his upper lip as he balanced the canteen cup with care to make sure he didn't lose a precious drop of his "medicine."

If my new friends were old enough to remember the war they had deliberately forgotten it. They were living in one of the world's most modern and economically strong nations. For most of them it was history—only history.

I was instantly a Very Important Person. With an audience of all the workers I was made an honorary member of the Helmstedt, Germany Post Office. They applauded as I accepted an insignia tie clasp, lapel pin and a patch for my shoulder. From the archives they found an old rendering of the building, as I knew it on my first visit. There was a struggle between emotion, pride, and my desire to be gracious as I accepted their gifts. Hoping to share this experience, I asked for three more renderings of the building. One was for Corporal Paul Kieffer, one for Sgt. John Spitzer and another for Staff Sgt. Everett Downing. Several months later I discovered that all three of my fellow soldiers were deceased and would not have the opportunity to "Return to Helmstedt."

Yesterday was forty-four years ago but today I was standing on the old stone bridge in the center of Maastricht, Holland. Its charm had been a casualty of war. The water, flowing beneath, arrived from somewhere, stayed a very brief period and departed to another unknown, just like that young solider I had been. Yes, it was time to remember.

Before I could remember being here I had to remember my road here. Maybe it had started on the farm, in the dairy barn, milking the cows before I reported to the army and basic training. Maybe it had started in the cellar of a troopship crossing the Atlantic. Most certainly it had started when this seasick soldier, with salt water oozing from his GI boots, walked ashore at Normandy's Utah Beach. Winter's snow and mud had halted the war and time spent in this small Dutch town was a three months' sabbatical from the sights and smell of destroyed armor, helmets that once belonged to living soldiers, the endless parade of supply trucks loaded with ammunition, food, and gasoline.

I left the bridge and walked toward Wilhelminastrasse, eager to see if the building where my squad had taken up residence was still there. Anxiety hurried my steps, and fear of disappointment held me back. The brick courtyard hadn't changed. The current residents invited me to see the basement where I had lived. I briefly sat by the wall where

I had been asleep in my bedroll and was awakened with the news that German paratroopers dressed in GI uniforms had landed in the area—the start of the "Battle of the Bulge." I walked slowly into the two-block boulevard area that was ours; it had belonged to the 39th Signal Battalion.

Memories, pleasant memories, caused today's summer sun and green foliage to disappear and be replaced by that fall and winter weather. The sights and sounds of forty-four years ago reappeared. I heard the sound of my boots on the snow as I walked my guard route on a moonlit night, and the rattle of mess gear as everyone ran to be first in line for mess call. And the squeaky voice of little Annie, the cutest four-year-old in Holland, shouting the vulgar curse words the GIs had taught her and then extending her hand to take the chocolate bar that was her reward. Two of my buddies, "Scrunch" Machek and lanky Charlie Allred, were wrestling in the mud and snow, settling an argument that had started with too much beer.

After two blocks of my yesterday, I entered the residential area where the family had lived. I remembered them: a mother, a father, a twelve-year-old son, a fifteen-year-old daughter, and Alice, seventeen, slightly more than one year younger than me. It would be ridiculous to try to find her. I didn't even remember her last name. A large red neon sign flashed "Honda Motors" from the front of the brick building that stood where their little home had been. I crossed the street and sat on the curb. Sitting on the curb, I could not recall meeting her but I did remember her family adopting me. They were proud to have me as a symbol of their liberation from the hardships of the German occupation. We had often sat in a circle in the living room and talked. I responded to questions about life on the farm, school, what our homes in America were like, and what I would do when the war ended.

During these times my friendship with Alice blossomed.

Our lives had been interrupted by war and for us future was a big question. War had become reality for me as a sophomore in high school. Alice was thirteen when German soldiers occupied Maastricht. We shared our dreams of life without war. She made me laugh, I met her friends, and we walked in the country. American films were already at the theater and we went to movies. I would have to keep it a lifelong secret from my Methodist parents, but we even went to a Catholic mass together. Were we in love? We were just two young kids, overwhelmed and confused by a terrible situation, finding comfort being together and believing that there would be a better tomorrow for us. We held hands, we hugged, and we dreamed of what life together might be for us.

But this was war and it started again with great fury. My squad followed the infantry across the Rhine River. War was a funny business—from the pleasant company of a remarkable Dutch girl, to crossing the Rhine with our own artillery firing from behind us, to digging a hole to find telephone cable that would provide communications to the beachhead. I don't remember how or whether we said goodbye. I did know that I was a soldier again and Alice was yesterday. As I left the curb and walked back across the street to the Honda agency I almost shouted, "God! It would be great to see her again."

Mr. Verhogen, owner of the agency, was interested in my story. After making a phone call he marked on a map the location of the city county building. Records of who lived in this location in 1944 would be available. The rest of my day was spent waiting outside offices, trying to understand the language and being referred to yet another person, in another office, on another floor. A friendly and understanding lady, speaking English and searching through a large record book, found the name of the person who had lived at that address. When she mentioned the

117

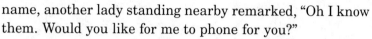

name, another lady standing nearby remarked, "Oh I know them. Would you like for me to phone for you?"

She handed me the receiver. My hand shook, I almost dropped it. If this was Alice what would I say? Would she remember me? "Hello," the answer came from a female voice in a friendly Dutch version of English.

"Hello, my name is Will Morris. I was an American soldier who was in your city in 1944. I am trying to locate a family that lived at...."

She interrupted, "This is Mrs. Verhogen from the Honda agency. You were at our shop talking to my husband this morning."

I had tried; it was best to move on. The next morning on my way to the train I stopped to thank the Verhogens. I was willing to abort the attempt to find Alice, but they were not. They had shared my story with Dan Smit who operated a music store on the same street. He was waiting to see me. Dan's father was my age and had lived in this neighborhood all his life. He had served in the Dutch army and had been imprisoned by the Germans.

Dan, his wife, and his father listened to my story. You would think, based on their interest, that I had liberated Holland all by myself. Dan had been seven when the Germans occupied their country. He remembered seeing both German and American soldiers. "Maybe this is not the first time I've seen you," he laughed. His father remembered the family that had lived there and thought that maybe they had a daughter named Alice. She had married Fritz Carten, who was a member of the city council, the very office where my search started and ended yesterday.

A familiar nervousness controlled my voice as I dialed and waited for Mrs. Carten's "Hello." Her name was Marie and she did not have a sister named Alice. As we talked, I decided to end my search. My enthusiasm had faded and even if I did find her, it could be disappointing. Why take a chance? She continued, "I have a friend that I have not seen for years. Her parents lived near that corner. She might know the family name. I'll call her. Can you call me at 6:00?" I agreed, even though it meant staying another day.

At six I phoned Mrs. Carten. She gave me the phone number of a lady who had lived near that corner. Trying to decide whether to call or just forget it and continue my journey, I walked to the train station and made a reservation to leave for Liege, Belgium at 11:30 the next morning.

Feeling it would be useless, I dialed the number. Another click of a receiver, a Dutch hello and my response, "Do you speak English," and once again I told my story to another stranger.

"That is where I lived. Alice is my sister." With a stumbling, breaking voice, for some reason all I could utter into that phone was, "Is Alice alive?"

"Yes."

"Where does she live?"

"We live in Zoonhaven, about thirty kilometers from Maastricht. But Alice is not here. She is on holiday with friends and won't return for a week. Is your name Bill or Will?"

"Will. It could have been Willie."

"Do you have a sister named Imogene?"

When I said "yes," she talked with great delight. "You gave us pictures of your sister, your mother and father. They are in our family album, and lots of pictures of you. How long will you be here? Alice will be so disappointed if she can't see you."

We talked for half an hour and after getting her assurance that she would give my best regards to her sister and extend my disappointment for not seeing her, I thanked her. Before saying goodbye she asked what time my train left and asked me to call her before it did. I agreed that I would call her at 9:00 the next morning.

My search had ended. At least Alice would be forced to remember me. The excitement of seeing her had not materialized but neither had the possibility of disappointment.

Morning was a new day and with all my traveling gear, I walked to the train station thinking about Belgium, Luxembourg, and even Paris. Standing by the "telephoon" booth at the station, I waited until my watch said 9:00 and dialed, waiting for my last goodbye, my last contact, my last memories of Maastricht. It was clearly time for me to move on.

The cheerful excitement in her voice surprised me. We talked like old friends. She wanted to come to the station and see me before I left. She had pictures she wanted me to see.

"OK, you'll recognize me. I'm six feet tall, have shoulder-length gray hair, will have a pack on my back, washed out jeans and a striped shirt. I'll wait for you right in front of the station."

"I'll leave right away."

Trying to be as tactful as I could with a lady, who wanted to see me more than I wanted to see her, I asked, "If you have a recent picture of Alice would you bring it? I'd like to see how she looks."

"Will! This is Alice."

Her sister had called her, and she had driven home overnight, from her holiday, to see me, and had been waiting for my 9:00 call.

I waited... looked at my watch, and waited. Every lady that approached could be Alice. When one whose appearance would have disappointed me passed, I was relieved. When one, who resembled what I wanted her to be, passed without looking my way, I was disappointed.

Then there she was. Without question it was her. It was

her smile. It was her walk. She walked directly toward me. I took off my pack, placed it by a post, and tried, unsuccessfully, to walk nonchalantly toward her. My hand extended and touched hers.

"Hello, Alice."

"Hello, Will."

I put my arm around her shoulder and we turned and walked to a bench. Facing each other, all we could do was smile. We either were afraid to talk or didn't know what to say. Years ago, our parting had been forever—yet here we were sitting on a bench in front of a train station just looking at each other in disbelief. Struggling to start a conversation I asked, "Tell me about your family, your husband."

"George was a classmate. Do you remember him? He was one of the friends we went to a party with when you imitated Hitler. He thought you were funny. He often remembered what you said. Do you remember it? Something about a black artillery soldier."

How could I forget? It had made her laugh and that pleased me. I shared with her again the story of that black artillery sergeant who, after firing a salvo at the German tanks, called out, "Mr. Hitler, count yo' men. Are you sho' they is all there?" I told her again how his devilish grin had emphasized his white teeth. She laughed, and that pleased me again.

We sat silently for a while before she continued talking about her family. "My husband had cancer. He died six years ago. We have three sons. They just bought me a new bicycle for my birthday. My sister and I ride every day." I told her about my family, my children, and grandchildren. She remembered my friend Wayne Stevens when I told her I had married his niece.

She asked, "Will, why did you come to Maastricht?" The arrival of my train interrupted my thoughts. It stopped at the station and left without one of its passengers. I shared a short version of my life, starting with Alice of 1944 and ending with Alice the elegant lady sitting on the bench at the train station. At that moment she was very special to me, and I sensed I was special to her.

We talked and talked and talked. We laughed about the joys of those three special months. Remembering them pleased her and it certainly pleased me. If she had answered in the negative it would have brought a cloud into a day of sunshine.

"Oh, I brought pictures from our album." She had pictures of my mom and dad, brothers and sister. I had given her a picture of myself playing a trumpet in front of our farmhouse. I was probably twelve years old at the time. And there were pictures of the two of us. We laughed about how young we were then. I felt like a teenager again.

The announcement of the departure of another train brought me back to reality. I looked at my watch. A few minutes of remembering had lasted three hours. She understood as I picked up my pack, put the strap across my shoulder, took her hand and walked into the station. From the window, as the train moved forward, I waved goodbye. She raised her hand in return. Her smile was gone and I felt a tear drop to my cheek. The train picked up speed and I sat wondering what Alice was thinking back there on the platform.

A few days later I was in my tent in a campground outside Paris. Heavy rain kept me inside. It was a good time to bring my journal up to date. I recorded my Maastricht experience and then wrote Alice a letter. I didn't record what I said to her but it probably went something like this:

Dear Alice,

It was a marvelous thrill to see you again. Our short time together reminded me of what an important part of my life you were those years ago. I am happy for your good life, and for your wonderful family. The miracle of seeing you again was as great or greater than our first meeting. I will always be proud that I have known such a grand lady, not once but twice.

May God bless you,
Will

When the rain stopped, I put the letter in the postal box near the campground. There was no return address on the envelope.

Ronald Kidd
January 1990
17

The tone, forcefulness and language of my remark surprised me. "What you printed in today's paper is a fat ass lie."

There was a moment of silence, and then Ron looked directly at me, hesitated, and softly, yet distinctly said, "Y-e-e-s-s."

His word, spoken in disappointment, lingered between us. He now knew that my opinion was based on personal knowledge and that he could no longer answer my inquiries without being challenged, yet I sensed that he wanted to continue our conversation. He would mentally position himself some place between defending the Peoples Government of China and telling this traveler the truth.

Two days earlier I had departed the sweltering climate of Malaysia, changed planes in Hong Kong, and boarded a China Airline flight. The Beijing airport terminal, unheated and without electric lights, was warm compared to the sub-zero snow-filled atmosphere outside.

My lodging was a small neighborhood hotel two miles from Tiananmen Square. My evening was occupied journaling my expectations of my visit to China.

When the Tiananmen Square riot and massacre took place I had been traveling in Brazil. The *International Herald Tribune*, a worldwide English-language newspaper, gave me my first account of the student massacre. The significance of this event had not registered with me because I was still too occupied with the mysteries of Brazil to think much about China. As time passed, however, my interest heightened. Most English papers I read during the next seven months carried editorial comments about the Tiananmen uprising. My curiosity grew more than my understanding. I wanted to go to China, but almost all stories in English language papers indicated that Americans were not allowed, or at least were very unwelcome, in China. In spite of these potential difficulties, my eight-month-old traveler's spirit said, "Go," and I did.

I was surprised to find the English version of the *China Daily* outside my hotel door the next morning and eagerly read it. Newspapers around the world, like children, are all the same and yet distinctly different. Reading the newspaper in any country gave me a first impression of the personality of that country.

An article in the morning paper caught my eye. It was dated January 24, 1990 and said in part that the United States Senate and House of Representatives had passed a bill called, The Emergency Chinese Relief Act, which prevented the forty thousand Chinese students studying at universities in the United States from returning to their own country to serve their homeland. Passing the bill by Congress was intended to support reactionary organizations for their activities against the Peoples Government. The Chinese description stated specifically that students were not allowed to return to their country. There was only harsh criticism of the United States Congress for being determined to devastate the efforts of the Peoples Government to make China the world's greatest nation.

My copy of the *USA Today*, which I had read on the plane from Hong Kong, described the potential United States law as an extension of Chinese students' visas to allow them to stay in the United States. The conflict in

Congress was over how best to allow the students to stay if they desired. President Bush had vetoed the bill and the Senate upheld it.

My tools for my first day's China adventure were a map of Beijing and a bicycle that I rented from an entrepreneur near my hotel. The Friendship Store was my destination. I had been surrounded by people for twenty-four hours but isolated from any form of fellowship, and it was time to search for another traveler. I needed mental support and encouragement to start what I hoped would be for several days, my China experience. It was cold, very cold, and snowing as I entered the street and joined Beijing's three million bicycles that move silently and in unison along the streets and wide boulevards of the flat terrain. Slowly, bracing myself against the frigid wind, I pedaled my bike the four miles to the Friendship Store.

From my journal I recall meeting Ron: "Now picture me in the coffee shop in the Friendship Store having coffee and trying to get cellophane off a hot dog when an English-speaking voice breaks the silence. 'I saw you come in and I should warn you that you probably should not eat that. It isn't good for a Western stomach.'"

What a treat it was to be with him. We sat at a table in a Chinese version of an American coffee shop located in the government-operated, tourist-supported, Friendship Store. A Scotsman by birth and education, Ron had come to China ten years earlier to help the *China Daily* start an English edition, and now worked as a journalist.

"If you want to see the real China you must visit the universities. And be sure you go to Shanghai." He talked with fascination about the beauty of both the country and the people.

"Do other foreigners work with you?"

"Not any more. There are thirty Chinese writers in my department who have studied in the United States and

England. They are able to help our people understand the world. We must understand the other great countries if we are to reach our own potential."

The conversation about the writers who had studied abroad caused me to ask about the conflicting stories in his paper and *USA Today*, on the visa bill. My question was guarded to disguise my true feeling as I inquired about the difference in the way the outside world depicted the subject. Our conversation continued for thirty minutes. It started out friendly, informative and lighthearted but shifted toward uncomfortable tension.

His answer was precise and canned. It was not the first time he had given this explanation to someone who questioned the reporting of this country's press. "Will, you have to understand that the Chinese mind is far different than the Western mind. Our writing is for the benefit of the Chinese. They understand this even though it is difficult for you."

I could not accept his answers. He was determined not to shift his position of defending the Peoples Government, which the paper supported. We were like two fighters in the early stage of the first round of a boxing match. Each was challenging the other, just to get a reaction, while taking great caution not to commit himself totally.

"Let's come back to what your paper reported. It is in conflict with the facts. What you say is different than what the *International Herald Tribune* reports, and it has nothing to do with the Chinese mind. It's what your paper reported that concerns me."

He relaxed, smiled, and went on to talk about the mix of educational and social standards of the Chinese population in an effort to ignore my concern. Talking in generalities, trusting that I would forget the question, he said, "Six hundred million of the one billion people who live in China are illiterate. In most cases they live in rural areas without the use of electricity or modern sanitary facilities." He went on to rationalize and conclude that for this group, combined with the better educated, and those who live in large cities, it is always in the best interest of the people for the media to present the news and information that the people "want to hear."

Here I was with a stranger, listening to totally unacceptable rationale for deliberately distorting the truth. Ron was trying to convince me that false information was in the people's best interest. I was inclined to drop the subject and move on but I couldn't. Our sparring had developed to a point of enjoyment for me, and it was my turn to talk uninterrupted.

"Ron, you read the *USA Today* and the *International Herald Tribune*, don't you?" His silent lack of denial allowed me to continue. "You and your paper know that the United States did not detain the students against their wishes. They were allowed to stay if they feared reprisal from your own government if they returned. Right? Why did you deliberately misstate the truth? And then try to tell me that it was what the people wanted to hear?"

We had now returned to compatible terms. We understood each other and the conversation continued. He explained their media procedure and policy to me. The article in question was credited to the official news agency, Xinhua. This meant that this news release was edited and approved at the highest level of the Communist Party. In effect, the party decided what the people should hear, and in this communist culture that meant accepting it as the truth. Silently, I thought about it and saw it for what it was: mind control.

For the next twenty-eight days I wandered around the People's Republic, Taiwan, and Macao. I listened and looked, always aware that these millions of people were told what to think; my belief that this was mind control increased. During this time the Soviet Union announced its willingness to give up its "sacred right," a one-party system. How did the Chinese government react? It published a document, "Opinions of the Central Committee of the Communist party of China on Persisting in and Improving the System of Multi-Party Cooperation and Politician Consultation Under the Leadership of the Communist Party of China." The *China Daily* was saturated with it. In simple terms it stated, "We thought of it first and decided last year that it was important to have opposing views." Last year in China was only thirty days ago. An English-speaking friend, Zhao Zhou Ran, with whom I had spent three evenings, assured me, two weeks earlier, that persons with opposing political views were discredited, relocated to remote parts of the country, and in some instances, put to death.

When I think of Ron, as I often do, I recall his statement that all of the college-educated writers who worked in his department would live in the United States if given the chance.

I asked skeptically, "Why?"

His answer was simple, specific and very direct: "Freedom."

Ron Kidd, the Scottish journalist who had been a writer for Beijing's largest newspaper for ten years, and I, sat at the table and talked. Actually he talked and I listened to his version of what really happened, up to, during, and after Tiananmen Square. It was January 6 and the Tiananmen uprising had taken place just six months earlier. It was an unbelievable story—if, in fact I could believe him.

"Will"—we were now friendly enough to address each other by our first names—"It is important to know that it was international politics, far more than the student uprising, that caused the young Chinese soldier to be executed by his own comrades."

His voice softened but remained firm as he continued, "Deng is an old man. He was returned to power, for the third time, in 1977 and is being pressured from within the party for control by younger men. To the Chinese mind, tradition and pageantry are important. Welcoming Gorbachev to Tiananmen Square would be the most important event in Deng's life. It would ensure him continuing as the party leader.

"Deng also coveted the prestige of having the world see the two greatest communist leaders soften their differences after years of conflict. This meeting would say to the world that communism will be the surviving government of all the powerful nations. Every world political leader would be watching and anticipating the effect it would have on the future of world politics.

"This event was of such importance that it could be seen on every television set in the world. Deng could not allow anything to prevent the world seeing this display of his greatness. Certainly not students who were asking for sanctions that the Peoples Republic of China had already determined were not in their best interests.

"Deng made the decision to remove the students by military force. He had dispatched a high government official, friendly to the students' cause, to address them. The official's words, 'I have come too late,' were unquestionably understood to mean that for now your cause is lost and you should disband for your own safety.

"The protest was already out of hand and the original leaders had lost control. The original group of students was very small. And they were some of the brightest in our universities. Their demands were reasonable and probably would have been granted if the uprising hadn't got out of hand. They wanted to choose their own course of study, the university that they would attend, and where in this large country they wanted to live and work.

"You must understand, in China the Party is responsible for improving the economic conditions to meet other great countries. They do this by programming talent that is needed and placing it where it is most needed for the good of the party.

"Students educated in the United States, England and Japan who have returned to China have had an immense impact on our education process and this influence would have caused these requests to be approved if other factors hadn't taken place.

"When the television cameras from around the world appeared, other students joined the growing crowd. They were protesting for the sake of protesting, not knowing why. The occasion became more important than the cause. As the protest grew in numbers, so did rumors of demands and it just got out of hand. As the anxiety heightened, more undesirables joined. The student leaders lost control of what had started as a very highly-organized, well thought-out, superbly-controlled expression of educational freedom. The protest became hysterical. When the students were asked to disband, there was no student leadership to respond.

"The entire world saw what happened. The communist leaders determined the revolt had to be crushed at whatever cost. Three army units moved into Tiananmen to remove 'the traitors to the party,' that had occupied the Square. There was a strict timetable for preparing the area in front of the Forbidden City for the arrival of Gorbachev and his welcome by Deng. No one knows for sure. Hundreds, probably thousands, were killed.

"Two days later the morning atmosphere surrounding Tiananmen Square and the Forbidden City was lifeless. The dismally-dressed Chinese who were moving about seemed to have no purpose in their activity. Maybe they were trying to understand, or perhaps totally forget, what had taken place in the past weeks. There was no evidence that the student spirit still existed. Bloody scars, resulting from the soldiers' gunfire, were very visible. The military force was nowhere to be seen. The soldiers were camped away from, but near, Tiananmen. It was here that the executions took place.

"At these campsites the Communist Party judicial system was in action. Soldiers were standing in silent, rigid formation. A lone soldier stood twenty yards in front, his back toward the formation. Their rifles were raised. The silence was broken by the sound of a single rifle shot that penetrated the atmosphere in a sharp, lingering, decisive sound. The bullet pierced the back of the head, just below the ear level, of the young Chinese soldier who stood all alone.

"Days earlier this soldier's trigger finger had frozen as his eyes saw the fear in the students' eyes. He lowered his gun, totally unaware that his compassion for young fellow countrymen would lead to his own death by firing squad.

"After the sound of the shot vanished, another sound erupted. It was the controlled cadence of the soldiers' voices, which burst into a thunderous roar. Their arms reached upward, extending their rifles, as they fulfilled their military obligation by celebrating the execution of one of their comrades, whom the political leaders had determined was a traitor to the Peoples Government. Perhaps part of them cheered because mind control or other circumstances led them to believe that they were in fact executing a traitor. Without doubt many of them responded from fear of reprisal if they did not fulfill this military duty."

This was part of Ron Kidd's story that day at the Friendship Store and I trusted that he believed that was what had happened. He indicated that the executions continued for several days as the government established their "truth" that the students were traitors and had attempted to destroy the Peoples Government. Any soldier who refused his duty to defend his country against these turncoats was also a traitor.

My fascination centered on his account of the early morning execution of a young, uneducated Chinese soldier. He had died as a traitor, just two days after the uprising. Ron desperately wanted me to know just who these young soldiers were. They were from the rural areas, totally different from what we were seeing in the city. They were part of the six hundred million inhabitants of China who are illiterate. The experience of being in the army and in such a large city was more than they could cope with—much less being asked to kill their own people. They didn't understand the student revolt and shared no feeling for its purpose.

From Beijing and my time with Ron, I wandered around China for another two weeks. I could not get my mind away from that young soldier. He was probably another farm boy—only a Chinese farm boy instead of one from Ohio. In the small villages and the vast countryside I saw where he lived, from birth, through childhood and youth, until the bullet lodged into the base of his brain.

As I traveled, often thinking about him, I named him Rho Wang, and in my imagination I wrote this story about his life:

He was not an only child, even though Chinese law prohibited married couples from having more than one offspring. The punishment of loss of job or demotion for having a second child meant little to his father. Likewise the promise of a paid vacation for having an abortion was meaningless to his mother. His father, a peasant farmer, wanted many hands to make light work in the fields.

Family life was simple, filled with long hard days working in the fields. His parents were contented and happy. They did not understand or care about the communist ideology. They only knew that their life was much better than that of their ancestors. They could raise their crops on government-owned land, sell a stipulated portion at a fixed price to the state, and then sell the remainder on the open market.

Education in the rural area was minimal. If Rho could read at all, it was only a few words. He did learn, however, some basic Chinese values. The family unit is supreme and should never be deserted. Having strong male offspring is both honorable and important to the parents. And most important is the respect for age. In China, age is wisdom. The judgment of the older is always superior to the younger. A father is always, regardless of education, wiser than a son.

Rho's transition from farmland to the life of a soldier exposed him to a different world. It was filled with obedience to military discipline, confusion, bewilderment, fear and a strong desire to return to the comfort and simplicity of the rural life. This ultimately led to Tiananmen Square and a traitor's death.

Rho was a soldier in the army unit that moved into the Square and opened gunfire on the students, not because of their resistance to educational policy and their stand for democracy, but because their presence in the Square had disgraced Deng at a time when the world should have been honoring him.

Much has been said in both print and picture about the bloody massacre that took place and the brilliant lives that were lost in the cause of freedom. Few people will know what took place back in the rural area where Rho's parents still tilled their farmland and where there was no knowledge of the renowned events at Tiananmen Square. The local official of the Communist Party came to the home of his parents with a very small, tightly wrapped box. Inside that box was the bullet that had been extracted from the base of their son's brain. His parents were required to pay the local leader a small portion of one yen, the cost of the bullet delivered to them.

The Peoples Republic of China would not pay the price for the execution of a traitor.

Pharmacist

February 1990

19

Lost in a crowd in Warsaw, I was just another Pole; in Paris I was just another Frenchman; even in Brazil I could have been a Señor. Blending in as a native in Shanghai was impossible. The other one hundred and thirty-eight passengers on the China Airline flight from Hong Kong to Beijing had paid little attention to me, but I was a foreigner on the streets of Shanghai.

This traveler had to admit that he had the flu. The transition from the tropics of Malaysia, to the sub-zero chill of Beijing, to the cold miserable rain of Shanghai, had taken its toll. I searched the Chinese Friendship Store, a store for tourists that will not accept Chinese money, until I found a large can labeled "San Francisco Del Monte, Grapefruit Juice." Trusting that the medical benefits of its vitamin C would produce relief, I consumed it during the night. Although restless from the dampness of perspiration and the chill of my room, I did manage some sleep.

One of fifty travel guides I used in my travel around God's Great Planet.

My travel book, *China, A Travel Survival Kit*, told me that Western medicine was sold at the Shanghai No. 8 Drugstore at 951 Huaihai Zhonglu. I located it on a map, decided I was too sick to walk, and waved to a taxi. My throat felt like an erupting volcano with each cough. I pointed to the location on my map and said, "Go here." The taxi driver rapidly bowed several times as he opened the door. My burning fever did not cause me to forget, "Always agree on the cost before your enter any foreign cab." I held three paper yuan, worth about thirty-five cents, and pointed at the spot on the map, and asked, "OK?" He shrugged, held both palms upward, and with a questionable look shook his head. I turned toward another passing taxi.

He quickly followed, taking my arm while he shouted in his Chinese version of English, "OK! OK!"

Opening the store door, I introduced myself with an attention-getting boisterous cough. Everyone looked toward me. They stared at a man a head taller than any of them, obviously not Chinese. No other customer was in the store. The sterile, but impressively neat and orderly, interior of this Chinese drug store was populated by, one, two, five, seven bright faces. Aware that I had entered the store, they each looked up from their work, nodded and smiled.

Rotating my face to make contact with each of them, I asked, "Speak English?" For a few seconds they shared glances and conversation with each other. The language I could not understand but their reaction told me the story. I was sick, I was where medicine was available but we couldn't talk to each other.

Thinking about what this morning would be, my fever and cough became less important as I mentally prepared for what would lie ahead. All seven of them, four females and three males, moved closer in a circle. They were in uniform, dark skirts or slacks and white blouses. The chatter among them, obviously about me, quieted and then stopped. They were in a state of pause, waiting for our encounter.

I held my head, leaned forward with both hands across my chest, took a deep breath, and looked for their reaction.

Two of them smiled. I coughed loudly, making sure that my body movements left little doubt that my illness was serious, and held my throat. Their reaction was positive.

More smiles and polite bows. These young professionals wanted to help. I held my forehead, placed my hands on each side of my face, frowned, and pointed upward. Yes, they understood. My new circle of friends smiled and bowed. These bows were from the waist and with very obvious respect for my illness. We were communicating and both the Chinese pharmacists and the old American farm boy were having fun. Everybody was smiling.

I walked to the counter, picked up a bottle of capsules, took out my billfold, and extended some money toward them. They understood. They walked away and formed a smaller circle near the counter. The change in the pitch of their voices, the nodding of heads and hand-gesturing told me they were asking questions and suggesting options. I was the subject of a Chinese druggist medical consultation. As I watched, I saw gestures, smiles, and questioning frowns. Their voices were a melody with pitch changes that evidently reflected their success or failure with their mission.

The consultation ended and a very attractive young lady departed and returned with a bottle of liquid. She placed it in my hand like you would tenderly place a baby chick in a toddler's palm. The label was Chinese language characters. After looking at it long enough to show my respect I returned it to her.

The audience, seven delightful young people watched in disappointment as I frowned and moved by head side to the side. She took the bottle from my hand, held it to her lips, and moved her head back, rubbed her throat and smiled. The absence of a positive response from me was greeted with a "we'll try again" smile.

A young man handed a container with the name

COFEL and the American firm PFIZER printed on it. The rest of the label was in Chinese. As I held it they moved closer and expressed pleasant enthusiasm for progress. They knew I was pleased but sensed my lack of confidence in whether this was the right medicine or not. That carton too, returned to its storage place.

Another huddle and consultation took place and then their serious conversation erupted with exuberance. They turned and watched, giggling with excitement, as one young man left through a doorway. He returned with a large carton with the brand name COFEL boldly printed on the side.

He lowered it from his shoulder to the floor and with deliberate precision lifted one smaller container after another from the case. As each one was removed their heads moved forward and their eyes were focused, looking into the larger box. Their eyes followed every movement he made. When the box was emptied he lifted a yellow paper. He had the prize. The others clapped their hands as he lifted it, gently unfolded it. He walked toward me and placed it in my hand in the same manner that I recalled the doctor handing me my newborn daughter.

All eyes were fixed on me as I looked at the paper and studied its format. The action now shifted to me and they waited in silence as I started my examination. The yellow paper was a printed description of the drug and the symptoms of the conditions for which it should be used. There were five separate columns, one Chinese, another German, then French, Spanish and the last column in English. I read the English column. This medicine was prescribed for high fever, chest congestion, sore throat, and general body discomfort. It should be taken every four hours with large amounts of citrus juice or water until conditions improved.

I looked up and smiled and gave the international

thumbs up sign that everyone in any nation understands. They reacted to my smile of success by breaking into spontaneous applause. They danced, they hugged and then they applauded again. A sound barrier had not been broken but the language barrier had. That half-hour of fun cost 7.8 yuan ($1.40 in American money). As I turned to close the door behind me, they encircled the entrance and were still bowing, smiling and bidding me farewell. I considered returning and giving them all a good American hug. I saluted them instead.

My health was so much improved that I walked the eighteen blocks back. Even though it was still raining in Shanghai, there was sun in my life.

Sight

September 1987

20

I reached for the phone, realized it was not yet daylight and struggled a sleepy, "Hello."

"Will, did I wake you? Larry, VPA. We have a possible pick-up at Bradford. Any chance you could go? Probably need to leave about six."

"What time is it?"

"Little past three. Weather might be a problem."

"Let me wake up first. What day is it anyway? Yeah, I'll go. I'll check weather and call you."

"Larry, it's Will, some snow north of the airport but I'm OK. I'll file a flight plan and wait at Allegheny until you confirm. Have the tower contact me. I'll be in 3071 Delta."

I identified myself to ground control as Life Guard 3071 Delta, and asked for flight clearance. The crisp, distinct voice confirmed, "Life Guard 3071 cleared as filed to Bradford, turn heading ninner zero, intersect radial zero six ninner to Homee intersection, victor 119 to Bradford. Do you have Bradford weather?"

Following procedures I repeated the clearance and confirmed that there was light ice accumulation above three thousand feet. The tower cleared me for takeoff. As I turned toward the first vector, the grey, wet clouds swallowed my little plane. Tower turned me over to Cleveland Air Traffic Control and I changed to the new frequency. Air Traffic Control asked if I had encountered any ice and I told them that it had started to form on the leading wing edge and the struts.

"This is my first time in ice. Might need your help."

"Looks like you have an important flight. Why don't you climb to five thousand? That should put you above the clouds. Let me know when you top out."

"Just passed through forty-two hundred and on top, clear and smooth. Thanks for your help. You guys and gals sure do care for us old men with limited time. Makes me feel more professional than I am. Thanks again, 3071 Delta."

The limited ice, although clearly visible and unbelievably concerning, had little effect on the airworthiness of my plane. It was a quiet, peaceful flight. The only interruption was from my friend, the controller, advising me that I was seventeen miles from the airport and that he would be leaving me.

Bradford was not a controlled airport—no tower—so I switched to the standard frequency and announced to the terminal personnel and any aircraft in the area, "This is Life Guard 3071 Delta, inbound fifteen miles west, downwind runway two seven." The belly of my aircraft kissed the smooth top of the cloud cover and then sank into it as the sunlight found another home. Shortly thereafter, the runway lights sparkled through the murky haze.

Flying parallel to the runway, before turning base and final, I could see several people following my path. Life Guard, probably the first arrival on this overcast morning, had piqued their interest. The squeal of the tires touching the asphalt brought my mind back to the task at hand.

As I taxied to the small terminal, an auto with a Red Cross on its door followed me to the tie-down area. Disguising my excitement by trying to look routine and professional, I removed the ice from the wing, and checked the fuel and oil for the return flight.

"Will Morris?" a man carrying a small white Styrofoam container asked. I signed a release, took the package and returned to my plane. It was still early morning and snow was filtering through the quiet gray atmosphere. A group of men with questioning expressions stood nearby and focused on the two of us. They must have suspected that this was not just a routine arrival and departure. Most surely they suspected that a human organ was being transferred from the small car to my plane.

I put the small white package on the rear seat and securely fastened it with the passenger seat belt.

All my audience turned and followed me as I walked to a pay phone. I advised the Medical Eye Bank of Western Pennsylvania that I had my cargo and gave them my ETA (estimated time of arrival) at Allegheny Airport.

Air traffic control cleared Life Guard 3071 Delta directly to Allegheny County Airport and assured me that no other aircraft would interfere with my flight. The humility of knowing that, if necessary, a jet would be asked to alter its course because the sky belonged to me was overshadowed by the thoughts of the package in the back seat.

I lifted from the runway, through the snowflakes, aware that a life somewhere in this area had ended. What were the circumstances—an accident, a fatal disease? Would the grieving family have any comfort with the knowledge that the tragedy of this life ending might be the start of a new life for someone who had not known the fullness of life?

The glow of the instrument panel contrasted with the gloom of the clouds that engulfed me. Then with a blast the plane broke from the prison of cold wet sky into the brilliant sunlight. In a few seconds I had moved from blindness to light. I was compelled to turn and see that package in the rear seat. The sun, with the absence of moisture, quickly melted the newly-formed ice from the wings. We—my little "putt putt" and me—skated across the tops of the clouds on a journey that now changed to a mission.

Thinking it, then humming it, and then expressing my unbelievable joy, I hummed Clara Scott's hymn. *"Open my eyes that I may see, glimpses of truth thou hast for me."*

At the Allegheny airport runway threshold, we left the brilliant sunlight and reentered the grayness. Because the weather limited my vision, just like a person with limited vision, I had to use other methods, instruments, to find my way to the runway.

After I taxied to the ramp, an agent took my package and left for the hospital. Before departing, he told me the eyes were scheduled to be in the operating room at Eye & Ear Hospital at 10:00 A.M., just six and one half hours after my phone had rung that morning.

Several days later I received a letter addressed to Will Morris, Volunteer Pilots Association, from the Medical Eye Bank, thanking me for my part in the sight-restoring process. The eyes had been donated by a forty-two-year-old lady and were used to restore the sight of a twenty-six-year-old man who had sustained a traumatic injury to his eyes. The letter concluded, "He is recovering nicely and his physician is very encouraged with his progress."

God's Language Barrier

March 1990

21

As my train moved from Seoul to Pusan my mind drifted back to 1957. I had chaired a Missionary Conference at my church in Bremerton, Washington. Our keynote speaker at that conference was Bob Pierce, founder of World Visions International. Years later this organization has received international recognition for ministering to both the spiritual and physical needs of the world's hungry. Its first focus had been on Korea and at that conference he talked about the boldness and vibrancy of the Presbyterian Church in Korea. My travel book, *Korea—A Travel Survival Kit,* stated that sixteen percent of the Korean population is Christian in a country which would otherwise be regarded as being Buddhist or Confucian.

I recalled reading about the Korean War. Pusan was the last holdout when the North Koreans almost pushed General MacAuthur's forces into the Korea Straits. A high school classmate of mine, then Colonel Bill Patton of the U.S. Marines, had been part of the invasion from the western coast, behind the North Korean lines, and prevented disaster for the U. S. military. It would be fun to visit Pusan and think about Bill Patton and see evidence of World Visions International.

It was Sunday March 4, 1990, when I found the large, modern Presbyterian Church in Pusan. Although the church bulletin was printed in Korean, I was able to understand that the primary worship service would start at 11:10 a.m. At 10:30 the worshipers were starting to fill the large sanctuary, which could probably seat six hundred people. A string ensemble was rehearsing, and I recognized the familiar melody of "Amazing Grace."

I was an unmistakable contrast to the neat classic dress and immaculate grooming of the Korean worshipers. My dress was dirty white canvas shoes, pocketed well-worn travel jeans, my favorite red, white, and yellow striped shirt, and hair that had not had a barber's attention in almost one year. A stranger, yes, but that melody from the organ left me feeling comfortably welcome and securely part of this Christian gathering. This changed briefly when the congregation rose for the singing of the opening hymn and I found myself a full head taller than the congregation, looking out over a sea of heads. Yes, I did stand out.

As the service progressed I could not understand a single word. My thoughts drifted to how a person with no eyesight must make greater use of his other senses. That was what I was doing. I watched the unquestionably talented choir director and the response of the vocalists to his leadership. I fancied myself at my church in Pittsburgh, listening to the rejuvenated choir that had been described in the "Spire," our monthly publication, and church bulletins that were part of my regularly-forwarded, but sporadically-received mail during the past year.

During the congregational singing, the choir director moved to the center, facing the worshipers, and virtually commanded them to raise their voices in a joyous singing response. The total congregation was participating in the worship service in a most enthusiastic manner. I recognized and in my own way participated in the singing of "Alas and Did my Savior Bleed."

What I assumed was the Morning Prayer was a quiet

peaceful time for me. I could not imagine what their prayerful joys or serious petitions were, but I silently shared my own. The congregation was hushed, and I assumed it was time for silent personal prayer. I thanked God for my good fortune of being here.

The sermon, by the standard of my church, was long. The minister was eloquent and forceful, quiet and engaging. Although I could not understand a word he spoke, I have never felt more a part of a worship service. I could hear the people hearing, and I could hear them thinking about what they were hearing. Because I was lost in the midst of this solemn, yet joyous, gathering, I was part of it and totally absorbed.

The offertory music was the string ensemble playing "Amazing Grace." I recalled the farmhouse of my early youth and could hear my dear mother singing, "Amazing Grace, how sweet the sound, that saved a wretch like me." I could never understand how an angel like Mom could identify herself as a wretch. Nonetheless, there in Korea, I sang the words silently from memory, and it was a beautiful meditation for me.

After an offering prayer, another hymn, and the benediction, the formal part of the service ended. What followed seemed to me to be recognition and awards for some church members. The congregation seemed to be happy and at peace with themselves and each other. Then the throng started to disperse, but not hurriedly. There was no urgency to leave their house of God.

My "church" had not ended. A sweet, short—hardly reaching my shoulders—elderly Asian lady seated to my left was aware of my struggles. There was little doubt to her that I was a stranger. With a smile she greeted me. I'll never know what she said to me, but I do know. She very politely bowed and warmly shook my hand. Although I couldn't understand her words she still communicated to me that she was indeed happy that I had worshiped with her and her friends. There is no question in my mind that the three words she uttered were "God Bless You."

As I departed the church the minister said, in English, "Thanks for joining us today." I walked out into the street, once again a stranger in a foreign land, knowing that I had been with dear friends and confirmed again without a doubt that there is no language barrier with God.

Another Audience

March 2004

22

Pittsburgh's Heinz Hall can be described as elegant or historic but certainly the description, "none other like it in the world," fits it best. My seat tonight was in row G—the seventh, in the first seat on the left aisle. My line of sight to the right of conductor, Mariss Jansons, focused on violist Isaias Zelkowicz and slightly to his left, one row back, was cellist Anne Martindale Williams. From my seat I could always enjoy the spirit and physical expression with which these two supplemented their music.

On the previous day Andrew Druckenbroad, the music critic for Pittsburgh's major newspaper, had described Anne's performance in the evening's last movement, "The andante, with its cello solo supplied warmly by PSO principal cellist Anne Martindale Williams, floated in gracefully. And Jansons imbued the finale with lightness and a tinge of melancholy."

The applause erupted; Mariss turned and faced the hall. As the sound swelled and the patrons rose to their feet, he graciously bowed and departed the stage. Returning, he gestured toward Anne, who rose to respond to the crowd's appreciation. At the conductor's direction she left her seat and moved forward beside him. Her tomboyish smile and blushing face were winning the hearts of this packed house. It was more beautiful, to me, than the music—and a moment that should just hang in balance for a time and not end.

Two patrons near the center of our row interrupted my

moment by moving toward the aisle, coats over their arms, and hurriedly departing. A sufficient number of others found heading for a trolley, beating the traffic, or being first out of the parking garage important enough to destroy the dignity of this moment. The applause that followed was divided between appreciative and polite. The evening ended.

The silence of the trolley ride home was broken by my wife's voice. "Will, you're quiet. What are you thinking about?"

"Warsaw. When I get home I'm going to dig out my journals."

As promised, my proprietor had breakfast on the table. There was a thermos of coffee, cream and sugar, bread, cheese, sliced meat and another piece of that good apple pie. This morning my destination was the Pan Am ticket office in Warsaw's Victoria Hotel. It was cold and raining and I was snuggling close to a large stone building to shield myself from the rain. While waiting for a streetlight to change, my eyes met a framed poster and I was sure that one large black word, although in Polish, was Pittsburgh. My gloom turned to exhilaration when I assured myself that it was, in fact, the Pittsburgh Symphony and that Lorin Maazel was pictured. And, could it be true, the date of the concert was today!

The line at the Pan Am ticket office, like all lines in Poland, was long—at least thirty-five people. It extended halfway across the lobby. Waiting in line, checking my airline schedule, killing what would surely be two hours of

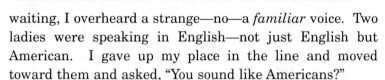

waiting, I overheard a strange—no—a *familiar* voice. Two ladies were speaking in English—not just English but American. I gave up my place in the line and moved toward them and asked, "You sound like Americans?"

"Yes."

"Where are you…"

They interrupted, "Pittsburgh, PA." Their husbands were part of the administrative staff of the symphony and, yes, they were in Warsaw for a concert tonight. The concert was completely sold out and had been for months. Spouses traveling with their mates, as a courtesy to the patrons, gave up their tickets.

The Pan Am ticket office lost its importance and the great stone hall that had sheltered me from the rain an hour earlier replaced it. At the Concert Hall office, by pointing at the sign, I somehow convinced a charming lady that I wanted a ticket and she somehow communicated to me that there were none. A man sitting at another desk occasionally halted eating an apple to help her understand me. He evidently understood English and helped her help me understand that any returned tickets would go on sale at 6:00 p.m. Language barriers are often somewhat overcome by body language and facial expressions, and I felt confident that her parting expression to me was, "You won't be attending the symphony tonight."

Lunch with a glass of wine made me drowsy, or maybe I was just tired. I returned to my little boarding house room and waited for six o'clock to arrive. I was getting realistic about the Pittsburgh Symphony and decided to call it a day. But staying in my small room until eight the next morning wasn't exciting, so I walked the twenty minutes to the concert hall. Three hours before curtain time I was in line, far back in line, for returned tickets that would likely never appear. Nonetheless I told myself, "I'm going to the symphony tonight." The thought of seeing a familiar face made me homesick.

No person in Poland wanted a ticket to this concert more than I did. No. That wasn't true. The fifty or more students, waiting in line for non-existent tickets, wanted to be inside that hall. They were university music students. I was merely a spectator. Hearing this symphony orchestra would be a highlight of their musical experience. Their excitement about the possibility was countered by the fear of disappointment if their hopes were not met.

An English-speaking piano student in front of me expressed this desire so vividly that I became more interested in securing a ticket for him than for myself. I asked him to hold our place in line while I tried to buy two tickets from the crowd entering the hall. The best seats cost 6,000 zlotys and 3,000 zlotys for the balcony, one dollar and fifty cents in black market money. I walked through the crowds that were moving toward the entrance holding a crisp $20 bill aloft in one hand and extending two fingers from the other, just like I had at a Super Bowl. These tickets were so sacred that my activity was degrading and insulting. I had been very offensive. The perception of Americans that the people of underdeveloped nations have: "I am rich, my money will get me anything I want," was clearly demonstrated. Ashamedly I returned to my place in line, knowing that I deserved the reputation that Americans have.

No tickets were being sold, and the line was getting longer. It was hopeless. I left my new friends in line and sauntered into the lobby where the guests were waiting. My eyes caught a distinguished looking man, unbelievably overdressed in a tan camel hair topcoat, who was handing tickets to other well-dressed people who approached him. I moved close enough to learn that they were speaking English. With nothing to lose, I approached him and introduced myself.

He was William Duffy, from the U.S. Embassy. After I assured him that I had indeed paid my taxes last year, I became the owner of two tickets for the Pittsburgh Symphony in Warsaw, Poland at 8:30 p.m. October 11, 1989. I went back to the line and looked for the piano student. He had become discouraged and left. I had missed seeing a frame of his life, and he had missed the concert. We both were losers.

My seat was in the last row, center balcony. The concert hall was in the architecture of years gone by. It was serene to be sitting there in the hushed crowd. The patrons would not allow conversation to interrupt the solemnity of this occasion. A noise to my right broke the silence. A door opened, and the students who had been patiently waiting in line quietly filed in and stood against the wall behind the last row where I was seated. There must have been fifty. I could not locate the piano student. The polite silence of this group spoke unmistakably and clearly of their appreciation for this good fortune.

A soft voice broke the silence and then was repeated in English. The bus bringing the orchestra from their hotel was delayed half an hour. The audience did not react. One sensed they had waited a lifetime for this, so what difference would thirty minutes be? It was just more time to relish the expectation.

The lights dimmed, the curtain opened, and there sat the Pittsburgh Symphony Orchestra in its entire splendor. They were a long way from my last row balcony seat but I searched and found that short blond hair, the blushing tomboy smile, the musician sitting with her prized cello. It was the Anne who had fascinated me with the story of taking her 150-year-old cello to New York for repair. She was not willing to trust it to the airline baggage department, but bought a first-class seat for it.

She looked across and into the depth of the darkened

154

audience as if she was searching for someone she might recognize. Little did she know that I was staring at the first familiar face that I had seen in one hundred and eighty-eight days. My excitement almost dictated that I jump off the balcony, race up the aisle, bounce onto the stage, and hug her.

The assortment of tuning musical notes quieted, the hushed audience waited in anticipation and then Maazel entered. The audience rose and welcomed him with a hearty, yet polite applause. The concert started. I turned to see the students standing against the wall behind me, only wishing that I could enter their minds and understand their thoughts.

I am not a student of music, but I enjoy being part of a group that delights in it. This audience was different. From my high vantage point, in center balcony, I could see their stillness as the music floated outward. They seemed to absorb every note and every movement with an intensity that indicated that it was passing, never to return, and they must relish it as long as possible. My excitement changed to awe about being here. I was part of something I could not understand but there was no room for lack of appreciation. It was a once-in-a-lifetime experience for me and, I sensed, for them.

Then this concert, like all concerts, ended. The audience rose, the applause was quiet and dignified. Maazel left, returned, left, returned, recognized his first violinist, his soloist, and the entire orchestra. The applause neither diminished nor swelled, but just continued. I glanced at my watch. It was almost midnight. The conductor returned and accepted beautiful roses. The night had ended, except not a single person left his or her seat. The dignified applause swelled, the orchestra would not depart.

Then there were a variety of short movements, more

vibrant this time, more dashing, and exciting, and more applause. As if to say to the audience, "This must end sometime," the sounds of "Stars and Stripes Forever" blasted into the air. The atmosphere changed. People were talking and laughing and applauding. The huge curtain closed across the stage. It was half past midnight and the joyous crowed moved toward the aisles and doors. I walked with them. It had been a special night for them and for me. In my journal dated October 11, 1989, I wrote, "I will never again, in my entire life, attend a symphony without my mind drifting back to tonight."

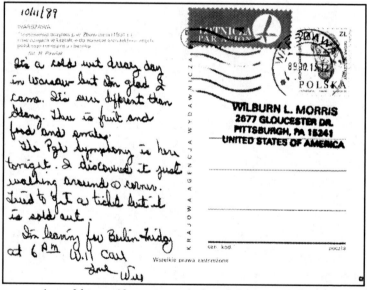

A card home. Always a reminder of that eventful night.

The Sign By the Road

August 2004

23

As fear and nervousness turned to a degree of confidence, I found myself taking inventory of my circumstances. There was no entanglement with lines, and I was not sinking at a rate that would lead to total destruction. In spite of this feeling of safety and the need to control the descent, I was momentarily disgusted with myself for having let an adventuresome spirit cause me to turn left at the sign that said, "Sky Dive. Come Fly With Us."

The big red arrow on the sign had directed me up a narrow country road to a small grass airport with an adjacent four-acre jumper's landing area. I had far more important pleasures awaiting me at my destination, so this was ridiculous. But now here I was, suspended in air, half a mile above the earth.

When I arrived at the airport, I had parked my car near the hangar, and with hesitation and reluctance, walked to the airstrip past a dozen or more youthful-looking people who were nonchalantly going about their tasks. Several were repackaging their parachutes on the dry grassy surface with meticulous care and concentration. Others were engaged in thoughtful conversation about their sport.

Walking to the edge of the runway, I looked upward to the sound of a plane that was climbing to a height nearing ten thousand feet. No one seemed to be aware of its presence until four colorful chutes appeared as specks in the sky. Ground activities ceased as attention focused skyward. I was the only participant that appeared excited

157

to see this colorful human display in the sky. The other club members were studying the four airborne members, who established different altitudes, and maneuvered to prearranged positions to practice their sport.

Most of the interest was on Sue, who was making her thirty-sixth jump and was known, on occasion, to self-destruct at point of touchdown. The other three landed, and Sue was skillfully maneuvering her oblong, colorfully-striped chute to the proper approach. She gracefully circled the landing area, positioned herself into the wind, and glided to a position about ten feet above the landing spot. She flared the chute, stopping the forward motion, and lowered herself to the surface with less impact than stepping off a curb.

What would it be like to experience this? Not for me! Maybe years ago, but this experience would escape me. Sue went about the task of repackaging her chute, and the others occupied themselves with what appeared to be a routine Saturday afternoon at a skydiving club.

I started to leave, but instead followed Sue—much more attractive after removing the outer colorful costume of the skydiver—into the classroom. Pretending that I didn't already know, I asked, "How many jumps have you made?"

She smiled proudly, "Thirty-six."

"What do you do when you aren't skydiving?"

"I'm a bank teller in Youngstown. My brother owns this airport and operates the skydiving club. He convinced me that there is more fun in life than standing in a teller's cage."

"Is it difficult to learn?"

"No, and it's fun."

"Any older students?"

"Oh, we had a man who was seventy." I was flattered as I imagined this charming young lady didn't think that I was seventy years old.

Her brother gave me a tour of the classroom, showing me the chutes, uniforms, helmets, and radio equipment. He failed to point out the sign, very visibly displayed in bold print, "Skydiving is a safe sport. However accidents and mistakes more normally lead to fatality than in other sport. This school does not accept liability for accidents."

Four hours of ground instruction led to the colorful striped nylon uniform, parachute on my back, helmet with enclosed radio for instruction, and a walk to the plane with a destination of five thousand feet above the surface of a four-acre field.

An instructor with a radio was in the plane, and another was on the ground with the same equipment. They were to be my monitor and tutor if needed in my trip from the plane to what I hoped would be a "step off the curb" in that small four-acre spot.

After confirming that the twelve-foot canvas line that would open the pack on my back was securely fastened to the floor of the plane, I stepped out onto the wing strut and, with trembling fear, released myself in the wind. The swinging motion that occurred softened the impact of the chute opening. But where was that four acre spot? It appeared behind my left shoulder.

"Will, you're looking good. You have about two minutes 'til touchdown, so let's practice the maneuvers."

I waited for more instructions, but they were not forthcoming. After all, it was my responsibility to test the skills that I had so recently learned in the classroom. I pulled a line extending from the right tip of the parachute and gracefully circled to the right. Likewise, pressure on the left line circled me in that direction. Pulling both cords attached to the front corners of the oblong chute increased the rate of descent, and pulling the two rear cords slowed the descent to the point of almost being motionless in the air.

"It's no different than flying my Cessna. I can fly this piece of nylon."

The voice from my headset abruptly interrupted my thoughts. "Will, you're looking very good."

At this point I felt like an expert, surprisingly confident. The only sound was total silence. There was no sensation of downward movement, only the earth rising to meet me. My confidence left as I thought about the landing and ashamedly admitted that, as a pilot, it is still a rarity when the wheels of my plane "kiss" the runway without a bounce. Maneuvering the cords, I descended as slowly as possible, more to postpone the touchdown than to enjoy the experience. Circling the landing spot, I confirmed from the windsock the direction of the wind and maneuvered into it for the glide to the soft grass. The position of the airstrip to the landing area allowed me to use it as a safety zone in the event I overshot the landing area—as I surely would.

I came down slowly and maneuvered with the slight touch of the lines until I reached an altitude about twenty feet above the surface—and then I panicked. My confidence was somewhat restored by the calming voice in my headset, "Looking good Will. Relax! Try to hold the chute at that level. It won't stall. Make sure your knees are relaxed, and be prepared to take a step forward at the first sense that you are on the ground."

Time, which seemed to be forever, passed until I reluctantly crawled from under the mound of nylon, horrified at facing the people who had witnessed my spectacular collision with earth. Spitting the grass and dirt from my mouth, nervously wiping the stain from my bright, borrowed uniform, and feeling humiliated and embarrassed, I gazed in surprise into the warm congratulations of new friends who had experienced my entry into and exodus from the sport of skydiving.

Visa Debit Card

August 1989

24

We had a lot in common. He was tall, thin, and had a pack on his back. He was probably another one of the many students spending the summer in Europe. I could hear his voice, speaking English, and it was easy to tell that his encounter with the bank employee had not been a pleasant one. He turned around, paused momentarily, expressing a gesture of disgust, and approached where I was waiting in line.

"Didn't go well?"

"No. All I have is a $100 American Express traveler's check. I'm going to the airport and don't even have money for a bus ticket. I don't want $100 in drachmas. The exchange rate at customs is terrible."

We did have a lot in common. We were both Americans, both travelers, and all travelers are friends. I gave my new friend the price of a bus ticket to the Athens airport and wished him well.

Waiting in line, I tried to forecast what experience would await me at that window. India and maybe Pakistan were my next stops. From what I had read, it wasn't likely that I could go to a MAC machine in Calcutta and get money. Admittedly, I was concerned and recalled my conversation with Ned Wellman, manager of my bank branch, when he counseled me on money needs for my travels. He had given me the confident assurance that, "Your Pittsburgh National Bank Visa Debit Card will be all you need. You can access your bank account from any place in the world."

161

"We do not accept Visa Cards," she spoke in perfect English as she reached for a city map and marked a route to another bank. A short walk later, and with a smile in my heart I saw the tricolor Visa sign as I approached the entrance to this bank.

"To get American dollars you must go to our main bank." Another route marked on my map, a streetcar ride, and a probing search led me to the massive, marble-floored bank lobby. The high ceiling, designed with Greek sculptures and supported by massive columns, left little doubt that this was the main office of the Commercial Bank of Greece.

After questions, referrals, more questions and more referrals, I found myself at a counter waiting to see a woman sitting at her desk. She was aware of my presence, but the newspaper she was reading took priority. Reluctantly she acknowledged me, left her desk, and walked toward my counter while looking up at the clock.

"It's closing time." Then just silence, waiting for me to react.

I waited, thinking, "No bank closes at ten minutes until two, and time is an abundant commodity in my life, so I'll play her game." With my bright tricolor Visa card in my hand I waited, and she waited for me to leave. I won.

"I'd like American dollars."

She took my card, reached under the counter for some paperwork, and asked, "How much?"

"One thousand dollars."

"Five hundred cash, five hundred in Cook's Traveler's checks."

"I'm on my way to India and I need one thousand in dollars."

Repeating my request did not please her. She had

stated her rules clearly and did not appreciate me questioning them. She reacted in a very authoritative manner—probably for the benefit of her audience, the other employees in the department. Raising her voice to a level that attracted their attention, she rebuked me and then again waited for me to leave. Those watching her smiled at her performance. She expected my immediate withdrawal but her audience was also my audience. They seemed to appreciate my calm indifference to her. She was on the defensive in front of her peers and kept repeating, while looking at the clock, "It's closing time."

Knowing when to admit defeat I attempted to tease her by graciously thanking her for her valuable time and courteous help and with my best smile turned and walked away. Without either direction or destination in mind and absolutely no need to rush to either, I surveyed this very impressive bank lobby. A very important-looking man at an important-looking desk caught my eye. I approached him, waited until our eyes met and then asked for assistance.

My adopted appearance often disguised my actual identity, and obviously trying to impress him with an importance that I neither felt nor desired, I explained that I was a retired business executive traveling and enjoying his great country.

Evidently he was impressed with my story. Together we went back to the counter I had just left. The same lady came forward with obvious respect. He talked; she listened. She and I now had an appointment at nine o'clock the next morning.

The next morning I remembered the toothache that I had tried to ignore for many weeks. A dentist across the street from my place of lodging had remedied it with a temporary filling. The toothache was gone this morning but somehow I suspected there would be a different ache today—the lady at the bank. I was determined to succeed.

Just take it one step at a time, stay unperturbed, and spend the day learning the Greek banking system. The episode would produce funds to finance my month in India and provide me with an education. After all, I was a traveler, and a traveler doesn't learn by listening and seeing; he learns by living the experience. It could and would be a good day in Greece.

Our courtesy and respect were obvious, if fictitious. First came an explanation that it was against the Greek law to give me more than five hundred U.S. dollars. The government did not want hard currency to leave the country. I understood that, but probably made a mistake in questioning her statement.

She summoned a bank official who explained it again. "You cannot take more U.S. dollars out of the country than you declared with customs when you entered."

"This money will be from my bank account in Pittsburgh, and my Visa receipt will verify that it came from outside Greece. There should be no limit on the amount I get." It worked. They made a phone call and returned to advise me that the thousand dollars would be available at their Visa office in another part of the city the next morning.

I had licked the system. Was American currency so valuable in Greece that a bank of this stature would lie to me? My mistake was that I was proud of myself.

At breakfast the next morning I took inventory of my plans, "My flight to Frankfort, where I change planes for Bombay, leaves at one o'clock the day after tomorrow. I'll get the money today, complete my journal in the afternoon, and then it will be clear sailing for India. Wonder what Christmas in India will be like?"

With confidence in my schedule I went to the bank's International Visa Section. After the routine "Good morning," I was greeted with, "There are not sufficient funds in your account."

"That is not true. I have my bank statement from last month." I explained to a disinterested woman what I had painfully learned in other countries. During the night computers in the United States are off-line being updated with the previous day's data. You must request funds during United States business hours. She was not interested.

After talking with her supervisor, we agreed on a strategy. I'd call my bank and ask them to send a wire authorizing the withdrawal. The wire would arrive overnight, and the money would be available the next morning before my airport departure. In their worldwide Visa directory we located the phone number of the Pittsburgh Visa Center.

I placed the call collect, knowing that it would be refused, and it was. After paying for the call, I listened with increasing irritation to the recorded message, "Thanks for calling Visa. We are here to serve you. Our office hours are from 8:00 a.m. till 9:00 p.m." When they opened at eight in the morning it would be three in the afternoon here, and the Athens banks close at two.

Back at my room, after four o'clock local time, I called my bank in Upper St. Clair, Pennsylvania. I placed a collect call to the bank manager. It would not be accepted but would surely get attention. It did, and I paid only after being assured that I could speak to the manager.

I visualized what was happening in that very familiar office of my local bank in Upper St. Clair. The manager was informed that he had a collect call from a Will Morris saying, "I'm in Athens." What a way to start his day.

"Who is Will Morris? See if we can locate his account."

Ned Wellman answered. He was the person who had assured me seven months before that the world's best method of financing international travel was to keep a small amount of U.S. currency and use a Pittsburgh

National Bank MAC Visa Debit Card.

He recalled our conversation, asked about my travel to date, and then listened to my attempt to tell him the saddest banking story he had ever heard. "I'm on my way to India and I don't have any money. PNC keeps telling the Commercial Bank of Greece that my account is overdrawn."

He interrupted, "Mr. Morris, I have your statement in front of me and it shows a $12,604 balance. The problem must be with the bank there."

"I know there's money in my account. You know it. But that vast worldwide computer network that you are so proud of doesn't work. I'm sorry. If you had been in my shoes the last few days, you would be frustrated too. It's my money, it's in your bank and I can't get it. If I get to India without money, I'll have a problem. My Visa card expires at the end of this month, and I left instructions for the new one to be mailed to the American Express office in Bombay—if I ever get there."

He recorded every detail of my request and repeated it back to me. The wire would go out immediately: the address was confirmed for absolute accuracy. The content of the wire was read to me for approval. An insignificant traveler who desperately needed a thousand bucks had brought two banking giants on opposite side of the Atlantic together. I had showed them.

Morning arrived and with my belongings in my backpack I walked to the bank to get my—yes, *my*—money. There was plenty of time, and my thoughts were more about leaving Greece than on the transaction.

A Mr. Pateo asked me into his office. He showed me the wire from Pittsburgh. I read it, exactly as Ned Wellman had read it to me, over the transatlantic phone seventeen hours earlier. They were to expedite my receipt of one thousand dollars in U.S. currency by twelve noon. My passport number was on the wire for identification purposes.

It was a document that any two human beings would have accepted but, "We cannot give you the money because your bank did not put an international authorization code on the wire."

"You must be kidding! Two of the world's largest banks, dealing in billions of dollars, and they will not give me a lousy thousand dollars."

All he would say was, "It's our policy." He would not listen to me. Again he repeated, "It's our policy."

It was Friday, and on Friday the banks in Athens close at 1:30 p.m. The Pittsburgh Visa Center, not my bank, would have to issue the code. It would not open until 3:00 p.m. Athens time. A phone call now would only get that recording again.

My flight left in three hours. Earlier in the week Pan Am had convinced me that the next available seat on the Frankfort, Germany, to Bombay, India flight segment was after Christmas. I couldn't call for the authorization code until Monday, and I wouldn't get money until Tuesday morning.

I left the bank absolutely and totally dejected. It wasn't the money. I'd find a way. Two banks and the worldwide Visa organization had done battle with a traveler, and it had been fun, except I had expected a different conclusion. I had never had a doubt, until now, that I would win. But the Commercial Bank of Greece had brought this traveler to his knees. Waiting on the street corner for a bus to the airport, I counted my money: 3,936 drachmas. After paying five hundred for the bus ticket my pocket still bulged with their money. At the airport, customs exchanged the balance of my Greek money, only after assuring themselves that it was less than I had on entry, for that good-feeling green stuff.

Airborne, I surveyed my economic situation: one well-worn $5 bill, two crumpled $1 bills, a soon-to-be-expired Visa card, and the unknowns of India. The flight arrived in Frankfort as scheduled. After passing through customs my eye focused on a bank kiosk with a Visa sign. That damn thing wasn't a friend of mine. However, I inserted my tricolor card, pushed a series of buttons, as directed on the screen, and asked this machine for one thousand American dollars.

Out came a receipt, no money: "Withdrawals limited to five hundred dollars. I tried again, asked for five hundred dollars, and out came five crisp one hundred-dollar bills. Holding them firmly in one hand, I made another pass at that machine and was rewarded with five more crisp, green, beautiful, spendable, one hundred-dollar bills.

And... on to India.

Five months later I faced the MAC machine in front of the Upper St. Clair branch of the Pittsburgh National Bank. For the first time in three hundred sixty-five days, I inserted my Visa card, put in my pin number, and asked for four hundred dollars. A receipt, but no money, dispensed from the machine. The receipt showed the balance in my account to be $2,912.65 and in rather bold letters the statement, "Withdrawal limited to two hundred dollars each banking day."

Thinking about Athens, my money, in my bank, but not for my use, I returned the tricolor card to my wallet. I turned to the door, opened it, and without invitation approached the stately looking desk where branch manager Ned Wellman was seated.

The Party

November 1989

25

It was more fear than nervousness. I had deserted, against specific instructions, the Finnish tour group, to wander Leningrad's streets. This was 1989, and the Russian Embassy would not grant permission for a private citizen to enter or travel alone in this country. It was clearly understood that I must be part of a group that was under the supervision of a government official. In all probability this was the best method of exploiting the lucrative, western-currency-producing tourist industry and controlling what outsiders could see in their country. An American teacher studying at the University of Helsinki had suggested that I join their Finnish tour to gain entrance. This was the only way that I had any hope of seeing Russia through the eyes of the people on the streets of Leningrad. I had decided to take the risk of staying at the tour hotel, leaving the tour and finding my own adventure, and returning to Finland with the same tour group.

Most of the day was spent wandering the streets and observing the visibly repulsive quality of life of the Leningrad inhabitants. It was beyond imagination that this country could have pioneered space exploration and developed destructive nuclear armament.

Nearing a business district, I approached what appeared to be a fine restaurant. Although it was not open, I walked into the dining room and was greeted by a man who had no understanding of English. A waiter who spoke and understood minimal English was ushered to my presence. He took me to a kitchen area, and he was able to understand, with some difficulty, that I was interested in dining that evening.

We went over his menu and as he spoke the items, I responded either yes or no.

"Pepsi?" I had already learned that Pepsi was the only American soft drink sold in Russia.

"Yes."

"Champagne?"

"Uh, Yes."

What the hell! I didn't know what I was doing or why I was here. Maybe I should leave and look at some more empty grocery stores. Or open wooden-shelved meat markets with very little meat and what was there populated with flies. And why should I be talking about champagne when just moments earlier a frail, poorly-dressed lady had pleaded with me not to take her picture as she stood at a counter in a dirty cafe eating soup.

"Salad?"

"Yes."

"Vegetable?"

"Yes."

"Chicken? Fish? Beef?"

"Yes."

"Dessert?" As he went on to explain the kinds of desserts, I interrupted with questioning gestures and an indication that he should decide.

He held up one and then two fingers, soliciting the number of people to be served. I frankly didn't know, but I responded by holding up two fingers and then all ten and shrugging that I didn't know. He seemed to be satisfied not knowing, and then pointing to his watch agreement was reached that dinner would be at 7:00 p.m. He gave me a card and painfully explained that my party and I could enter regardless of the crowd waiting at the door.

Back at the Leningrad hotel I enthusiastically recruited companions for my "non-tourist" dining experience. All were people that I had met on the train ride from Helsinki to Leningrad. Our party included Ken Uselton, football coach at Visalia Junior College in California, and coach of a semi-professional football team in Helsinki, and Jim Hansen from Salt Lake City, who was playing linebacker on Ken's team. Jim had played with the Pittsburgh Steelers in 1986-87. Brent Osborn from Humbolt State in northern California was a runningback on the Helsinki team. Ericka Steffens, grandma to us all, came from Vancouver, British Columbia, with her twelve-year-old grandson Adam.

The eight of us, in two taxis and with joyous expectations, left the Leningrad hotel for our night out. I had arranged the affair and played the role of the trailblazer. Grandma Ericka was our college dorm housemother: "Have fun but be good." The three football guys were out for a good time. They had had enough visiting museums and taking boats up the river to last them for a lifetime. Adam, our twelve-year old grandson escort, was insurance that we would keep the night honorable. He did question why the taxi drivers went into a dark alley when we asked them to sell us black market money.

There was a large crowd waiting at the entrance but the card the waiter gave me entitled us to enter immediately. We were ushered to our table at the edge of a circular dance floor. It was the only empty table in this festive nightclub setting.

My friend, the waiter, was proud to have us as "his guests." We seemed to be the only foreigners. There were about two hundred people in the room and their conversation reflected anything but seriousness. The music played, the people danced, our pepsi and champagne, all eight bottles, arrived and was consumed. Conversations began with the neighboring table, and the increase of alcohol in the bloodstream definitely diminished the language barrier. We laughed and sang, even though we didn't know what we were singing. "Grandson" Adam, enjoying the surroundings, drank more and more pepsi and gazed in wonderment.

It was good to be here. We were having fun, and I for one was glad that we were not back at the Leningrad Hotel with the seven hundred guests eating their tourist version of a Russian dinner. They were probably talking about their wonderful tour guide—you soon learn from tourists that all tour guides are wonderful—and talking about the government buildings and the magnificent art in the museum.

The occupants at a table near us were celebrating a birthday, and the guest of honor, a middle-aged lady, spoke a little English. A friendship and bonding developed, and our two parties of eight became one party of sixteen. Language, cultural, political and economic differences didn't exist. We were no longer strangers. We had been accepted as people, just people. Except for our eight new friends no one knew we were from the West. We had become, if only temporarily, part of Russia.

Adam, our grandson, temporarily shirked his responsibility of keeping the party honorable. He let the coach Ken Usleton leave our immediate group. The coach found a partner and called her "Tiger Eyes." She was stunningly beautiful, and after each dance, he returned to our table and assured us that he was falling more and more in love. This continued until he returned with the pronouncement that her price was one hundred American dollars and laughingly suggested that he might sell his Levi's jeans on the black market or have us each contribute ten dollars to help him pay for the experience.

The food had been consumed, and the party seemed to be winding down when seven glasses of vodka, a gift from the neighboring table, were delivered to our table with the suggestion that we drink a toast to the honored birthday guest. We responded by drinking the toast, singing "Happy Birthday," in English of course—and ordering a round of champagne for all. The round we ordered turned out to be eight small bottles, so we drank lots of toasts. We must have toasted birthdays, anniversaries, weddings, Columbus discovering America, Russia's entry into space, and who knows what else. Let there be no doubt that Russians, at least these Russians, are great consumers of liquor, and at this time we just didn't want to be different. The band stopped playing their lively music at 11 o'clock— that is until Grandma Erika, who also was having a good time, enticed them to play for another half hour for one American cigarette each.

My friend, the waiter, brought our check. It was written in English for my benefit. Sixteen bottles of champagne, ten Pepsis, eight salads, eight steaks, eight deserts. I added a very generous tip and paid the check with black market money that I had purchased from the cab driver. The party had cost me the equivalent of twenty-four U.S. dollars.

The evening was over. The entire crowd left their tables, briefly mingled together, and moved toward the exit. A strange incident took place. It was strange, for me, because in my culture it would have attracted a lot of attention, but here it went unnoticed by all these people. A very physical controversy took place on the opposite side of the dance floor between two men. One was left lying on the floor, and I assumed he was temporarily unconscious. The crowd continued toward the exit, and he was left without even the slightest interest.

Moments later another fight erupted as we passed. One

man was on the floor being kicked in the face by the other. Still no interest from the crowd. At the foot of the stairs, as we walked out onto the street, two more men were fighting. One fell to the ground and appeared motionless. Two policemen, or soldiers, directing the crowd, did not respond in any way to the incident. It was just as if it hadn't happened. I moved between the two large football players, knowing they knew the way home.

Grandson Adam, completely full of Pepsi but very alert, suggested we ride the subway back to the hotel. The modern escalator took us three hundred feet below street level where we waited along the graffiti-free, marble wall for the train. After traveling under the Leningrad river, we surfaced near our hotel where the many air-conditioned busses were waiting to take their tourists on trips to the museums, to the ballet, up the river to Peter the Great's castle.

Grateful that I was a traveler, not a tourist, I walked to the hotel. In my room I tried to visualize the economy and quality of life that existed in this country where twenty-four dollars would buy an evening's dining that probably would have cost eight hundred dollars in Pittsburgh.

In the bathroom I looked for a glass to have a drink, before remembering that in Leningrad's finest hotel the water was not fit for human consumption.

George

August 1989

26

I boarded "The Orient Express" in Vienna, Austria. Its journey had started in Paris and stopped here to take on passengers. The next destination was Budapest, Hungary. Sliding open the door of the first-class compartment revealed three passengers finishing their uncomfortable night's sleep in a space designed for six persons sitting upright. Their silence, lack of acknowledgment of my presence, and refusal to make eye contact left little doubt that they were not anxious to welcome another passenger.

They remained rigidly fixed in their somewhat reclining postures. The presence of a tall man with long gray hair and a cumbersome backpack looking for quarters did not please them. Their stony quiet clearly declared, "Close the door and search for another dwelling place." But my beachhead was established, and I refused to retreat from their silence. Their traveling belongings and a lady sitting near the window filled the seating to my left. She stared out the window at the passing station, refusing to acknowledge my presence. Across the aisle a lady, larger in stature than her older companion, was just as protective of their space. The man who instantly reminded me of comedian George Burns looked up and extended a restricted but friendly facial welcome.

I moved inside, removed my heavy backpack, and very carefully secured it in the only space available, a rack between them and above their heads. The man smiled an expression of appreciation. He apparently was pleased with the painstaking details of my knot tying, which provided a degree of security from a falling backpack. They made no effort to adjust their seating arrangement to provide space for me. The motion of the train made it difficult for me to hold my balance, so I collapsed between two of them.

Oh well, I was aboard and on my way to Budapest.

We sat in silence until the blast of wind from a passing train rocked our car. It was loaded with military armor traveling in the opposite direction. After the quiet of our sparring for space came the first sound from this petite man. "Russian tanks!"

Conversation started, or at least "George" started talking. His knowledge of the political unrest in the USSR and the potential effect of Gorbachev's journey through Russian history impressed me. Like every other traveler in August of 1989 he had strong interest and opinions about the future of the Russian people. He would ask, "What do you think," pause ever so briefly, and then answer for me. There was no room for disagreement.

His traveling companion kept busy doing nothing. She unenthusiastically tolerated his conversation, which she had probably heard many times. The very brief and sporadic conversation between them had a special blend of respect, cool tolerance, and yet warmth. They were an unusual couple.

I was pleased; another adventure, with a couple from New Zealand, whose spirit and zest for adventure had permitted them to wander around the world. He was eighty-seven and she was seventy. They were travelers, not tourists, and we were on the Orient Express from Vienna to Budapest.

He was very British. His charm was the balance of his dignified ego and brilliant mind, which he constantly, and purposefully illustrated. He had employed his traveling companion to live in his home and care for him after the death of his wife of fifty-five years.

"Is she traveling as an employee or are they sharing their life?" I wondered. Regardless, at this point in time their residence had changed from a grey cedar shake house on the leeward side of a green hill in New Zealand to the adventures of today's world, and I was a guest in their compartment on the Orient Express.

Conversation continued. "Were you in England? How do you feel about the monarchy?" All one question.

"Yes, in June," and as I paused to consider a view, which I didn't have, I already knew he would oppose it. It was his unique way of enjoying conversation, which he always controlled. And I enjoyed it. We were in conversation, even though he was always on the podium.

It was time for a smoke, and in spite of my suggestion that he enjoy it in his window seat he honored the regulation of this non-smoking car. He declined to smoke in the compartment, but the corridor was different. And... out there, I suspected, he could "kick up a fuss."

The compartments are on one side and the corridor on the other on European trains. The hallway is a bustling, crowded environment. Passengers who cannot afford a compartment or find a seat in the overcrowded coaches, stand, holding the window rail to protect themselves from the motion of the moving train. People moving to and from the lavatory weave through the continuing confusion of passengers.

His small stature rose to prominence as he lit his cigarette, slowly and deliberately inhaled, held his breath, and then with great satisfaction and enjoyment, exhaled his lung's contents into a rising cloud. Perhaps not, but almost assuredly, he had directed this rising haze toward the face of an American. His western hat, gold chain around his neck, wide western belt and expensive-looking western boots identified him as a self-impressed tourist. Looking down at George with an air of supremacy, the tourist announced, "This is a non smoking car."

"Only the compartments," came the, I-dare-you-to-continue, gentle but sarcastic reply.

"Smoking cigarettes will kill you."

"I'll enjoy them while I'm living. How old are you?"

"Fifty-three." By replying, the American was on the defense, and my new friend was back in control.

"I'm ninety, been a Boy Scout for seventy-three years. Started smoking at fourteen." Then silence.

His rival, realizing that the audience surrounding them was not sympathetic to him, tried to reestablish control of the scene by debating the point that even though he was not interested in preserving his own health, he should have consideration for others. He did gain control, but only because the man with the cigarette in his hand wanted it that way. The other riders were enjoying his performance. He was enjoying aggravating this prideful, intimidating American tourist for the pleasure of his audience.

The train rolled on, and we returned to our compartment. These two were truly fascinating. She cared for him like his mother. He responded in appreciation for her attention while rejecting the care he felt he didn't need. His temporary irritation always melted into tenderness. There was fondness and appreciation that they had initially attempted to hide from me.

As our friendship and trust developed, the four-hour trip seemed to pass in thirty minutes. Our style of conversation changed. Listening and learning from the others' views on economics, government, theology, geography, and lifestyle enriched us both.

When we said our good-byes in Budapest, I felt enriched, having met one of the world's special people. He was George Burns in many ways, refusing to get old, always searching.

I walked through the train station thinking, "In twenty-three years I will be eighty-seven. I hope my mind will be as active as his. What an example of growing every day."

It was noon when the train arrived. In three hours I had exchanged a limited amount of money, and found a residence in a private home. Feeling secure with my arrangements for the night in a new country and culture, I walked back to the train station to get a map and find out the location of the post office and police station, where I was required to register within twenty-four hours. And of course, what had by this time become my favorite hobby, buying some black market local currency.

The government tourist office was located in the train station, where I could get my map. I was startled—no, shocked. What were the chances of this happening? Mrs. George was sitting on her luggage with George nowhere in sight. I was delighted to see her, and she was relieved to see me after the three-hour separation. Her first words were, "I told you he was too stubborn for his own good. He is in that line waiting all the time to go through official channels to get a place to stay."

She was extremely concerned for his well being. I waited with their luggage while she went inside. She returned saying he needed a drink but they did not have any local currency. I gave her a one hundred forint note, and she bought two orange juices and two sandwiches. I took the food and drink to George.

"Mate, it's sure good to see you."

I stayed with their luggage, entertaining myself by bargaining with the black market moneychangers, so they could wait in line together. I felt good about myself. They had befriended me by allowing me to share their compartment. Now I could repay them with my own friendship.

When they exited the tourist office with a big smile, he was lighting a cigarette. I helped them take their luggage to a taxi and again waved "so-long" to my friends.

I took their picture with their camera as they entered the cab. I heard George muttering that he needed a gallon of beer and was ready to go out for the evening. "Mrs. George" replied, "I'm too tired."

Walking to my residence, across the bridge and up the hill, I thought about those two marvelous people and particularly George. My one hundred and thirty-eighth day bumming around the world had been a good one.

I didn't even know their names.

Ephesus

October 1989

27

Extremely relaxed and with "no place to go," I gazed out the window as the outdated bus bounced down the country highway south of Adana, Turkey. The bus stopped at an intersection, and my eyes focused on a small directional sign: E F E S - 1 kilometer. An arrow at the bottom pointed to my right.

"Ef-fa-sus." I tried to pronounce it and ponder its familiarity. "Ef-fa-sus, E-fe-sh-ains. Is Ephesus in Turkey? It couldn't be. Thessalonica, Corinth, Sparta. I thought all these places were in Greece. Only one way to find out." With my pack on my back and following the dusty tracks of a two-wheeled cart, pulled by an overburdened donkey, I walked toward the ocean.

"Only one dolla, very good su-ven-eer, how much you give?" The aggressive vendors surrounded me. I wanted to strike out at them. "Don't you understand? I'm a traveler, not a tourist." Temporarily, I accepted this retail circus and purchased a dozen post cards showing the ruins of Ephesus.

"Who would be most impressed with me being here?" The greetings I scribbled all started:

"Dear _____, I am in EPHESUS." They were addressed to my wife, my children, older grandchildren and of course all four ministers of my church.

The commotion of the peddlers' circus pleasantly disappeared as I walked through a gate and down the narrow winding road toward the city, half a kilometer away. I stopped and gazed at the ruins of this ancient city in the valley before me. "The Letter to the Ephesians," written by Paul from his prison in Rome, had been delivered to this very spot. A combination of nervousness and excitement swallowed me as I moved on down the hill to walk the streets where Paul had walked on his third missionary journey fifty years after the birth of Christ.

To my right was Arcadian Way, leading to the now silt-filled harbor. The scriptures had described this as a great city, the center of commerce and culture, with few equals anywhere in the world. Today it was uninhabited, remarkably preserved and silent—stone silent.

Lost with my thoughts and unaware of my walk, I found myself sitting on the top rim of the huge stone amphitheater. Far below me, in the center of the stadium, the soft melody from a string quartet invaded the silence. Sounds of their music floated upward like the smoke from a fire of burning leaves on an autumn day of my boyhood on the farm in Ohio.

My interest was Paul. I sat on the ledge, high above the floor of that great amphitheater and thought about him. Challenging my memory of the biblical account of his letters, I stood beside the hated tax collector as he was "giving approval to his death," as Stephen was stoned until his life ended. And near Damascus, I saw him blinded listening to the words coming from a void, "Now get up and go into the city, and you will be told what to do." If only I had studied and could recall more. But I did know that the letter he wrote to the people of this city had been miraculously preserved, circulated, and studied by millions for its meaning for their lives.

Now I could hear the string quartet again. It was time to experience Ephesus and look for Paul.

I walked down the stone street to where the harbor had once flourished. There, in my imagination, I met Paul and quietly walked with him through the city.

He walked ahead of me and stopped at a gathering and began to speak. As he talked, more people stopped and moved closer. I could hear his words, spoken with confidence: "I became a servant of this gospel by the gift of God's grace…" I waited, they listened, and when he had finished, they quietly departed—not alone but in smaller groups. As they walked away, the movements of their hands and heads disclosed the continuing discussion of Paul's inconceivable message of grace.

Shouts came from the stadium entrance. People rushed through the gates. Not like the people that had listened to Paul on the street, these were boisterous and disorderly. I went through the gate with them, but Paul waited outside. Demetruis, the silversmith, stood before them and yelled.

"Men, you know we receive good income from our business. Paul has led astray large numbers of people. He says man-made silver gods are no gods at all." The craftsmen and workers shouted their approval. Paul had escaped their fury by waiting outside.

The city clerk came forward and spoke, calming the crowd. "If you have a difference against anybody, the courts are open." He stood silently as the unruly crowd calmed, turned, and dispersed.

And Paul joined me again as I walked on. One moment I was placing the sole of my shoe exactly on the spot where his foot had been, and the next moment I could hear him walking beside me. "What if there had been no Paul? Would I and millions of others throughout the world be embracing our faith?"

We passed the Temple of Serapis, Angora, and turned into Curetes Street to the Baths and then through the streets lined with formidable stone structures that would

183

last for centuries and centuries. We came to the city wall, and I exited through Magnesian Gate. Paul remained inside, and I returned to my world.

I walked that kilometer along the country road where I could find another bus "going no place."

It was a typical Sunday evening and I was touching base with my kids and their families who all live in different parts of the country. Tonight Stan, my eldest son, who lives in Corvallis, Oregon, and is part of Hewlett Packard's management team, described a three-week business trip he was planning. The first stop would be France, then a few days in Germany, and then on around the globe for a week at a manufacturing plant in Taiwan. His last stop would be three days in Singapore. I began to think, "I can't believe what has happened to my four children. What champs they are." My thoughts were interrupted by a different tone in his voice.

"Dad, I've been traveling a lot, and it's been tough on Patty and the boys. I'll be in Singapore when we celebrate our twentieth anniversary, and I was thinking." He hesitated, maybe to allow me to prepare myself for what was coming next. "I was thinking if there would be any way Patty could come to Singapore, we could take a three-day vacation before I come back to work's rat race. I have plenty of frequent flyer miles to get her there, if you could see yourself clear to come out and stay with the boys." Silence, and then, "They would be a handful. They're almost as difficult as I was for you, but there was only one of me."

"You know how to challenge your old man, don't you? Yes, you always did and I guess you always will. Let me give it some thought and touch base with Mom and I'll get back to you."

I flew to Portland, Oregon, where Patty and the boys met me. She boarded a plane for San Francisco and Singapore, after going over the daily routine for each of the boys. "They understand they have to follow this, but they will still give you a bad time." She was more nervous about leaving her boys with me than about her trip. I didn't know then but later realized why.

The ride home was pleasant. The boys were already celebrating both Mom and Dad being absent from their lives. I unpacked and moved into the master bedroom and took time again to admire the home that Patty had designed and had built when they first moved to Corvallis. The sunken conversation room with fireplace was not like any I had ever seen. It would be good to spend time alone there and read.

Determined to get my babysitting duties off to a good start and establish my grandfatherly authority, I started with the first day's bedtime checklist. Colin, age seven, informed me that he was allowed to watch television before he went to bed, even though his mother had given me instructions to the contrary. Brian, age thirteen, wanted to talk with a friend on the phone, after the time his mother said was lights out, and Jason insisted that he was allowed to stay up until eleven. And this was only the first night. For the next five days I heard, "Dad lets us do it. Mom says we can do it." Only the dog, Billy, respected my authority without question.

The mornings, afternoons, and evenings, taxed my nerves and patience. The boys simply ganged up on me. "We're allowed to go to the mall after school." But my instructions were that that was a no-no. "It's OK with Mom if we stay at a friend's house until bedtime." My instructions were that it was homework at home. The more I tried to be the loving grandpa, the more demanding they became. I started counting the days—no, the hours—until Stan and Patty returned.

During the day, while my grandsons were at school and I was alone thinking about that night's strategy to maintain peace and calm, I also found myself thinking about their dad when he was their age. When their dad was Colin's age, he had been diagnosed with epilepsy—the grand mal version. It had been the beginning of a very tough life for him. In 1956, medicine had not been able to control his seizures. Although most of them happened at night while he slept, they occurred enough at school for his classmates to consider him a freak. It was a cruel time for him. I recalled his tearful words, "When they choose up sides for games at school nobody chooses me." I remember wondering what he was thinking when others were looking at him and talking about this weird kid, while he stood alone. It was not a pleasant environment for a young boy in his developing years.

When he was his son Brian's age, he was suffering because my work required the family to move to Sacramento and then Napa, California, and on to Bellevue, Washington in less than four years. Three new schools in three new cities provided him little opportunity to create friends and develop confidence in himself. The less desirable, undisciplined crowd, who needed followers, accepted him, and these were certainly not the ones he needed to be with. Our assessment of our quality as parents was at it lowest when one evening a car with his unruly friends stopped in front of our home. We went out to greet him and found him lying on the lawn with his face bleeding from a beating those young thugs had given him before depositing him there.

When Stan had been Jason's age, we lived in Pasadena,

California. He was doing well and his academic standing after his sophomore year in high school was almost honor category. His medical condition would not stabilize. Driving was important to a sixteen-year-old but California refused to issue him a driver's permit because of the medication he was taking. At the start of his junior year he really applied himself to his studies, but the seizures intensified. The best analysis of his medical condition determined that the pressure of studying to achieve good grades was a major cause of the seizures. His doctor's words were, "You need to decide whether grades or health is more important." His mom and I decided.

His health was protected by the wisdom of that decision but it gave him justification for lack of discipline and not applying himself. Not accepting responsibility became his full time occupation. He did learn to drive but could not drive alone. During his junior and senior years he was a disciplinary problem at school and at home. The school psychologist advised us the best recourse was to let him make mistakes and pay the price for the decisions he made. I was not prepared for his advice concerning Stan's acquiring and drinking beer. "Let him drink beer until he is drunk, pass out in the gutter, wake up and not be able to find his way home. Let him suffer for the decisions he makes. He'll respond better than trying to follow what you want him to be."

These were difficult years and father and son were often at odds. Without question, health—although completely controlled by medication—was an issue. His refusal to apply himself caused me pain. His bitterness over not being able to drive appeared to be a big factor in his attitude. I agreed with him that the State of California was forbidding him his right by not authorizing a driver's license.

Thursday was the next-to-last day of school in his

senior year at Pasadena High School. Graduation would take place in the Rose Bowl the following night. The two city high schools and Pasadena City College would have a combined ceremony, with an expected attendance exceeding 25,000. It would be an experience that families and friends of the graduates would rate above the colorful New Year's Rose Bowl games, which made this great stadium famous. There was only one little problem at our home. Today, the faculty would decide whether Stan's academic standing would warrant graduation, or whether Mom, Dad, Sue, John and Dave would be in the stands witnessing what could have been.

His mother and I prayerfully discussed how we could help our son. Not being able to drive at age eighteen was a real handicap, and we decided to remedy that. He went to Phoenix and lived with a relative, got a job, established residency, and got an Arizona driver's license. With my permission, he did not reveal that he was an epileptic. He selected a new VW, which I bought him for his high school graduation gift.

With a driver's license in his pocket and a VW with shining Arizona plates decorating its front and rear we started the joyous ride back to the Golden State. Entering the outskirts of the Mojave Desert, we stopped and bought a yellow plastic dishpan and a gallon of orange juice. He was the pilot; I asked no questions, which pleased him. The next stop was the ice machine at a motel. He invented and installed an air conditioner in his new car. The dishpan, heaped with ice cubes he had borrowed from the motel, not only kept the orange juice cool, but cooled the air that flowed from the vent and upward to refresh the two passengers. My oldest son was a complete person with a new auto and a creative air conditioner. We were returning to Pasadena where he would start college. We crossed the desert, drinking the refreshing orange juice, and were truly father and son.

His tenure at Pasadena City College was brief. He never revealed whether he was asked to leave or just quit. Short-lived employment in an electronics plant was followed by another job. Our family relocated to San Francisco. He worked as a forklift operator, making what I thought was too much money for his own good. Somehow we agreed that he would attend Linfield College in the small rural town of McMinville, Oregon. It was an immediate, although short-lived, success. Blinded by early results I agreed that he could join the local chapter of my college fraternity. Big mistake: declining grades, declining attendance and then no college at all. Knowing whether he or the college made the decision that he was not academic material would serve no purpose.

As parents, we decided that Stan had to be on his own. We recalled Pasadena, when, as a fifteen-year-old he had disappeared and we had no knowledge of his whereabouts. After an evening of tears, we decided he was in the Lord's hands. We again left it that way. Positive signs began to appear. He loved to ride his bicycle with good fiends. When his sister, Sue, left for college in Spokane, Washington, he put her luggage in his VW, handed her the keys, and bid her good-bye. Leaving the next morning on his bike he rode 1,000 miles to Whitworth and returned home with his bike in the back seat. Each night on the bike ride, he phoned to tell us his whereabouts.

Somehow he ended up in Eugene, Oregon, worked part time, and enrolled at Lane Community College. He studied woodworking with the idea that after community college he wanted to go back to college and become a teacher of that craft. On a business trip to Oregon I spent an evening with him. He had applied for and received state welfare, had purchased an old trailer near school to live in, and was doing OK. He cooked dinner for me that night and shared with me that he had attended a Basic Youth Conflict conference in Eugene led by Bill Gothard, a well-known Christian psychologist. Even on his limited budget he had purchased two tickets for us to attend when the conference was in our area—probably telling us that, in his judgment, his parents were the problem. Bill Gothard had impacted Stan's life.

There was an eighteen-year-old girl in Eugene who also enjoyed riding bikes. She studied secretarial skills at the community college. She invited Stan to her church youth group and he started to attend with her. They rode their bikes to school together. One day Stan disappeared and Patty became concerned. With her mother they went to his trailer and found him suffering with a very high fever. He had not taken his medication and was not in good shape mentally or physically.

Patty and her mother took him home and Mother Harbour nursed him back to health. She says, "It was fun to watch them fall in love." The wedding took place March 11, 1977. I watched them drive away for their honeymoon on the Oregon coast in the VW that now had legal Oregon plates on it.

We know that many people had an effect on Stan's life: As parents, we probably did more than we were willing to admit. Bill Gothard, Mother Harbour, and scores of others—including one very special person, Patty. Stan and Patty moved to Hayward, California and Stan enrolled, seriously this time, at Hayward State College and studied computer science. They rented a little house that was on ground condemned for highway construction. They rented the basement to two students for enough to pay their own rent. It was a thrill to visit their little home.

Patty worked in the admissions office using skills that she had acquired at Lane Community College, and with that income along with a reduced tuition because her husband was the student, put Stan through college. He graduated debt-free. Just prior to graduation, the *Hayward Daily*, the morning paper, featured a full-page store about wives who put their husbands through college. Patty, complete with pictures and her story, was the feature of this article.

To celebrate graduation from college, they put their bikes on top of the VW and headed for Vancouver, British Columbia. They left Vancouver, riding their bicycles across Canada to Buffalo, NY and then on to our home in Murray Hill, New Jersey. The trip had been long in planning. As parents, we agreed to have boxes to ship their bikes back home, and our graduation gift would be their plane tickets. In our family room we had a map marked with their route. When we received a phone call telling us their location, another pin with a little flag went in the map.

They arrived twenty-three days later. Actually we went to meet them, and with our auto lights flashing and horns honking, escorted them the last few miles of their 2,726-mile ride. After the arrival festivities subsided somewhat, we suggested we go to the basement to see the boxes we had purchased for shipping their bikes home. We had two little boxes on the roof of a new red Toyota we had purchased for their college graduation gift. They looked stunned—not realizing that the car was their gift but wondering how they were going to get their bikes in those small boxes.

A week later the shiny red Toyota with two happy kids inside and their bikes on top left our driveway. That former six-year-old epileptic, who had had to overcome a lot of obstacles, thanks to his wonderful wife Patty, was heading to a bright future that brought career success, parental success, and spiritual success—and brought Grandpa to babysitting to those uncontrolled but wonderful monsters who were now asleep upstairs.

I walked outside, past the Jeep parked in their

driveway, around the powerboat they used for water skiing, looked back up at the home Patty had designed, and walked out to the curb to see the twenty-year-old Toyota that was still part of the family.

Rae Elizabeth Pugh

November 1997

29

One of the thirty-seven death announcements in the *Tacoma News Tribune* read:

Rae Elizabeth Pugh, born November 13, 1898 in Everett, Washington, died Saturday, November 29, at the age of 99.

Rae was the daughter of pioneer educators Roswell and Emma Dell Friars. The family settled in Tacoma in the early 1900s. At the end of World War I she married her childhood sweetheart, Vivian E. Pugh. Later, due to his disabling illness, she embarked on her business career. After working during World War II in the personnel department of Todd Shipyards, in 1944 she became personnel director for J. C. Penney in Tacoma.

She is survived by her daughter and son-in-law, Elizabeth and Myles Barrett; three grandchildren, Gregory, Ann, and Michael Barrett; five great grandchildren, Alexander, Kenric, Owen, Myles and Marissa; and a nephew, John Friars. She was preceded in death by her husband and her brother and sister, Clarence and Lola Friars.

At her request, there will be no services. Memorial donations may be made in her name to the Mary Bridge Children's Hospital, 317 Martin Luther King Jr Way, Tacoma, WA. 98405. Arrangements by Mountain View Funeral Home.

That obituary notice in the local paper was a generic, factual account of Rae Pugh's life, but there is much more to tell. In September 1947 my new bride, a nursing student, accepted a six-month scholarship to study tuberculosis in a government Indian Hospital in Tacoma. I took a semester sabbatical from the university I attended and we moved West. Finding temporary employment was difficult and the best I could find was washing dishes from afternoon until midnight at the Poodle Dog restaurant in a small community near the hospital. The pots and pans, steel wool, and dishpan hands motivated me to look for another career. I ventured downtown to the department stores. This was a big step because a farm boy, recently a WWII soldier, typically wouldn't lower himself to work in a store. As I gazed across the street at the yellow and black sign "J. C. Penney," I recalled as a young boy listening to a conversation between my father and a neighbor. They were sawing and cutting firewood on a snowy day in the woods near our farmhouse.

"Oscar, you've got a new pair of shoes." Having new shoes during those depression days was not an everyday occurrence. "Where did you get them?"

"You'll never believe it. I bought a pair of shoes at Penney's a couple months ago and the right one always hurt my foot. We went to town Monday and I went to the store and asked them if they could stretch the right one. Just thought one foot was larger than the other. They looked at both shoes and said one shoe was one size smaller. They gave me a new pair of shoes, even though I had worn them for two months and they had dry cow manure all over them."

Recalling that story and with a new impulse of confidence I decided to look for employment that might improve my status as a dishwasher. I did not own a coat, so with my wife's raincoat over my arm I entered the store and met Mrs. Pugh. After some conversation we went to the manager's office and I became an "associate." My six-month temporary job lasted thirty-eight years.

I'll always remember—because I can't forget—Rae Pugh. Until I retired, I always addressed her as Mrs. Pugh. Our association was six short years but her presence was an important part of my life for thirty-eight years, and even beyond.

The store was a closed union shop and I was required to join the Retail Clerks Union within thirty days. I didn't join because I did not want to and couldn't afford to. At the end of thirty days Mrs. Pugh called me to her office to inform me that Saturday would be my last day because I had not complied with the employment agreement. It was Thursday and I had two days to comply. I confided to her that I didn't want to join a union. She understood and respected my feeling but went on to explain that it was not her decision but a binding contract between the store and the union. I shamefully admitted that even if I would join I didn't have the eighteen-dollar initiation fee. This gracious, beautiful, understanding lady opened her purse and gave me eighteen dollars. I repaid her three dollars each payday.

At least twice, in confidence, I recall her suggesting that I needed a haircut. The discouraged look on my face suggested that I didn't have the funds. When payday came I repaid her for the price of improved grooming. I was a nobody in the organization, and she was top echelon but she wanted me to look like she wanted me to be.

Fritz Sanders, a decorated World War II Infantry Captain, returned to his home in Canyon City, Colorado where his wife taught school. He reentered the family meat packing business. His wife brought home a book that she thought he might enjoy. It was Mr. Penney's biography, "The Golden Rule." Fritz was so inspired by what he read that he left the family business and went to New York, where he graduated from New York University with a master's degree in retailing. The company assigned him to its Tacoma store as a trainee and I, now the manager of the infants and girls department was his supervisor and responsible for his training. During the next two years, we, and our families, became close friends. Nancy cared for Ruth when our first son was born, and Ruth cared for Nancy when their daughter was born.

But there were storm clouds. In spite of his enthusiasm, my close friend was not in the right business. It was apparent to me that he should be terminated and encouraged to go into another field. Mrs. Pugh counseled me, and rehearsed the techniques for this unbelievably difficult task. The separation took place, and both our families' lives continued. Fifty years later we are still close friends. Fritz and Nancy live on Mercer Island in Lake Washington. Their lives have been very fruitful. Two children graduated from Yale, and years after the termination I watched his yacht go through the Ballard locks from Lake Washington to Puget Sound.

Years later, I realized that Mrs. Pugh saw something in this insecure farm boy that I didn't know was there. She wasn't teaching me to release a personal friend; she was helping, insisting, that I grow. And I guess I did grow because I continued to accept responsibilities that were far too great for me. She was always the second person I called, after my family, when I received a promotion or new assignment. For the next thirty-eight years there was always a part of Rae Pugh in me and in my interaction with other company colleagues.

On June 25, 1985 the J.C. Penney board of directors concluded their resolution accepting my retirement with the following:

The legacy Will leaves, therefore, is not one of documents and programs that bear his name. It is a legacy of careers and lives that he has influenced and strengthened.

Any credit given to me would have to be credited doubly to my friend Rae Pugh. If my life did in fact touch others it was because she touched mine. She is a special, a very special, "accident of my birth."

Sharing my retirement plans with Rae Pugh.

It was kinda out West, along the lazy flowing Colorado River below Parker Dam, Arizona. The air stream from the southbound motor homes rocked my little auto as I left Emerald Canyon and looked for a watering hole I had frequented three years earlier.

Playing golf at Emerald Canyon had reawakened some of my aging muscles and left me weary and in need of refreshment. The taxing greens and the challenging fairways that nuzzled in the narrow canyons of the desert mountain overcame my exhaustion. The transition from shoveling snow from my driveway in Pittsburgh to sunburn on the desert golf course had taken three days. The Blue Water Indian Casino with its bright neon lights was totally out of character in the tranquil Western countryside.

On down the road, located in a small unimpressive shopping area, the Paradise Café appeared just as it had earlier on a similar midwinter excursion. Inside the door was a large birthday card wishing "Casey Adams" a happy birthday. A brass spittoon, waiting for contributions to honor the occasion, was centered in front of the card. I remembered Casey, a cowboy guitar player and singer. His presence assured the bar and dining area would be flooded with locals. It was good to be here again. Although no one acknowledged my entrance, I felt at home in the familiar surroundings.

The sun had already departed when Casey arrived. The boisterous and fragmented sound of "happy birthday" exploded as he entered. Tall, slender, mustached and smiling, he looked every bit the western part he played. He was, without question, a local hero. Vicki, the bartender, responded to my narration that I had been here three years ago by "slightly" remembering me. "I'm not concerned about the kind of scotch, just the amount," caused her to insist that she remembered me.

Nonetheless, the ribs and the soothing drink set stage for the music and merriment that permeated the surroundings. Casey Adams, whether a stage name or actual, fit his character. He entertained with either a guitar or banjo while singing or playing a harmonica held in front of his mouth by a frame on his shoulders. He was truly a one-man band—that is, until Homer arrived. Homer was both shorter and wider than Casey. His flat leather western hat, although striking, did not overshadow the generous stomach that taxed the support quality of a white T-shirt to its limit. He carried a banjo at his side.

Homer, obviously known to most of the patrons, announced his presence by saying that his wife had gone to a wedding so he came to practice. For the next hour we were blessed with the rousing sounds of many versions of the song "Dueling Banjos," by two dueling banjos. Each segment of this pleasant music started and ended with Casey singing, with unbelievably authentic expression, "I'm Just a Plain Old Country Boy." It rolled from his throat, it bounced from the rafters and it engulfed all surroundings. Maybe thirty people at and adjacent to the Paradise Café bar were captivated by being in the presence of smiling, fun-loving, fabulously entertaining Casey Adams, just a plain old country boy.

One thing was certain: a gray-haired, seventy-six-year-old man, satisfied with the lingering taste of barbecued baby back ribs and mellow with the scotch, sat at the bar, comfortable with the knowledge that he was a plain old country boy watching these people pass his window.

It was time to remember some of the yesterdays of my life. Casey would provide the background music. I remembered that, not old enough to attend school, I had dreamed of riding in an airplane manufactured in the neighboring community of Middletown, Ohio by Aronica Aircraft. Joyce, older than me, shorter than me, and more wrinkled, managed the Kofa Inn in Parker where I was now staying. She was a native of Middletown, and her husband, now deceased, had worked at the aircraft plant. She described her first ride in that little cloth-covered tail dragger plane, and I remembered my unfulfilled dream. Aware that the music still filled the air, I remembered watching those same little planes from Middletown leave the grassy fields between the hedgerows of France and fly over the German lines as artillery spotters during the second World War. What brave men those pilots were. And I knew that if my country had not asked me to serve in that war, I would not be sitting at a bar in Parker listening to a guy named Casey sing about being a plain old country boy. Gosh! I was glad to be there.

My own life's motion picture, already started, continued to roll. Sitting at a bar in Parker, Arizona, reflecting on the frames of my life's journey, I remembered. It was 1948 when I had worked undercover with Dave Beck, founder of the Teamsters Union, to settle a labor dispute in Tacoma, Washington. My skin turned to gooseflesh as I recalled having dinner with Mr. James Cash Penney in Colorado Springs. Pennsylvania's Governor Thornburg's relaxed and friendly presence caused me to feel important, and we discussed business in his office in Harrisburg for half an hour. Sophia Loren, the Italian actress, could never imagine the number of times I would relate to friends that I had dinner with her in San Francisco. And friends my age, still ask as they gaze at a picture on my den wall, "Is that Doris Day with you?" Bob Michael, minority leader of the U.S. House of Representatives, after a couple of drinks, was on stage in a Mississippi restaurant singing "God Bless America." I sat at a nearby table and led the applause with his political enemy and personal friend Tip O'Neil, majority leader of the U. S. House of Representatives. And on November 7, 1982, Ruth and I were invited to the White House for a visit and dinner with President and Nancy Reagan. Not bad for a country boy.

Once again, "Just an Old Country Boy" filled the air. Vicki replenished my drink, surely suggesting that I return from my party to theirs. Momentarily I did, only to gaze at the patrons, and wonder what frames of what lives they were enjoying.

The sky was so clear, the moon so bright, the quiet desert mountains so alive that I rode back up the road to my motel with my headlights off, just being alone in a wonderful world. At Casey's birthday party, back down the road, I had been impressed with important people that I had met. That was not the Will Morris that I was or wanted to be. The people that I was most honored to know were just ordinary to the world, but not to me. They were special, very special, because knowing them was what had enriched my life the most.

In the quiet of the night, totally unaware of where I was, I remembered a fellow soldier who had a picture of the infant daughter that he had never seen, displayed in our tent. The inspecting officer, Lt. McDonald, stating it was not military, told him to remove it. Sgt. Spitzer, standing at rigid attention, slowly responded, "Sir, there is no man important enough to make me take that picture down." The officer's response, "As you were," erased the tension of the seven soldiers in the tent. Just an ordinary soldier—but to me he was a giant.

No one in my world knew Hattie Reed. She was just an

ordinary math teacher who entered and left our world without fanfare. I am probably the only person that will ever know of her greatness. Nothing in my college experience taught me to understand a problem before you attempt to solve it, but she did. I can still see her standing over my desk and hear her words, "Wilburn, first explain the problem to me."

I remembered when my sister called to advise me that her husband had died from a heart attack. She and her six children asked that I conduct his funeral. Uncle Dwight was *only* a truck driver to the world. In preparation for the service I took a slow walk along a meandering stream and recalled my memory of him. Phoning each of his children and asking, "Tell me about your dad," left little doubt that he was truly a one-of-a-kind parent. His children and their children are a testimony to his greatness and I was privileged to know him.

Uncle Marion, my sister Helen's husband, already knew he was terminally ill with cancer as he responded to one of many awards he received for his pioneer efforts in the international field of growing corn. Just out of high school he had borrowed money, bought machinery, and rented land to start a career that would take him to both China and Russia as an expert in that food-producing commodity. To most of the world he was *only* a farmer. To me he was a giant, and I was privileged to know him.

And that list of ordinary people went on and on. The question entered my mind. Why are ordinary people such special people to me? In the quiet of that night it became clear. God had planned this farm boy's life and it was just my role to discern and follow His plan. These were the people that He had planted to enrich my life. Knowing his Son had made all the difference. No longer was I important. The "I" became part of God's plan, and my talents became gifts to be used for whatever outcome pleased God. All the wonderful blessings in my life are gifts from God. I have been blessed, primarily, by *ordinary* people.

I silently walked to my room. The next day, like all my days, I would be going around the next corner.

Will Morris was born in Ohio, in 1925, and became an author in 1988 by keeping journals during his trip around the world. He lives in Pittsburgh, Pennsylvania with his wife, Ruth.

Who among us wouldn't wish for ourselves the kind of retirement that Will Morris has enjoyed? In 1985, after a long and accomplished career with J.C. Penney, Will embarked on a second career that included interacting with college students, church pastors from across the country, and a multitude of ordinary but unique people. He became a world traveler. Now, more than 20 years later, Will is still traveling his retirement journey and, lucky for all of us, he took a lot of notes along the way. The result is this engaging memoir, *Around the Next Corner*.

Tom Costello
Publisher